"Hebrews 11:1"

"Faith is our

Women of faith

from the Old Testament

by Mary Davis

"hope"

the**good**book
COMPANY

Women of faith from the Old Testament
© Mary Davis/The Good Book Company, 2005. Reprinted 2010, 2014, 2017.
Series Consultants: Tim Chester, Tim Thornborough,
                    Anne Woodcock, Carl Laferton

The Good Book Company
Tel (UK): 0333 123 0880
Tel (US): 866 244 2165
Tel (int): + (44) 208 942 0880
Email: info@thegoodbook.co.uk

Websites
UK: www.thegoodbook.co.uk
US & Canada: www.thegoodbook.com
Australia: www.thegoodbook.com.au
New Zealand: www.thegoodbook.co.nz

ISBN: 9781904889526

Printed in India

CONTENTS

introduction: good book guides

Every Bible-study group is different—yours may take place in a church building, in a home or in a cafe, on a train, over a leisurely mid-morning coffee or squashed into a 30-minute lunch break. Your group may include new Christians, mature Christians, non-Christians, mums and tots, students, businessmen or teens. That's why we've designed these *Good Book Guides* to be flexible for use in many different situations.

Our aim in each session is to uncover the meaning of a passage, and see how it fits into the "big picture" of the Bible. But that can never be the end. We also need to appropriately apply what we have discovered to our lives. Let's take a look at what is included:

⊖ **Talkabout:** Most groups need to "break the ice" at the beginning of a session, and here's the question that will do that. It's designed to get people talking around a subject that will be covered in the course of the Bible study.

⊕ **Investigate:** The Bible text for each session is broken up into manageable chunks, with questions that aim to help you understand what the passage is about. **The Leader's Guide** contains **guidance on questions**, and sometimes ⊗ additional "follow-up" questions.

⊡ **Explore more (optional):** These questions will help you connect what you have learned to other parts of the Bible, so you can begin to fit it all together like a jig-saw; or occasionally look at a part of the passage that's not dealt with in detail in the main study.

⊡ **Apply:** As you go through a Bible study, you'll keep coming across **apply** sections. These are questions to get the group discussing what the Bible teaching means in practice for you and your church. ⊡ **Getting personal** is an opportunity for you to think, plan and pray about the changes that you personally may need to make as a result of what you have learned.

⊡ **Pray:** We want to encourage prayer that is rooted in God's word—in line with his concerns, purposes and promises. So each session ends with an opportunity to review the truths and challenges highlighted by the Bible study, and turn them into prayers of request and thanksgiving.

The **Leader's Guide** and introduction provide historical background information, explanations of the Bible texts for each session, ideas for **optional extra** activities, and guidance on how best to help people uncover the truths of God's word.

why study Women of faith?

So, what's this series of studies all about? Women clergy? Nuns? Saints and martyrs? Actually, none of these. *Women of Faith* investigates eight women from the Old Testament—women who, despite the differences of time and culture, had the same ordinary lives, common hardships, and unforeseen crises that we experience. They lived in a world with the same problems as ours: selfishness, greed, jealousy, cowardice and the many other failings that spoil our lives today. They experienced the same sort of doubts, discouragements, griefs, bewilderment and lapses into sin that we do. And the same almighty, holy, loving God, who intervened in their lives, still speaks to us today.

Despite the fact that the documents of the Bible were written in male-dominated cultures, in every epoch of history covered by the Scriptures there are important accounts involving women. Their actions and experiences play a significant part in the great overall story of the Bible—the relationship between God and humanity, and God's purposes in sending Jesus Christ to our world.

We look at these eight women in the order they appear in the Old Testament, to get some idea of their place in Israel's history. While one of these is an idealised character (the wife of Proverbs 31), the other seven are real, historical characters. They are certainly not perfect paragons that will simply defeat and discourage us. Nor are they merely ornamental "props", spicing up the Bible with a bit of female interest, but with nothing useful to show. Between them they represent a whole variety of backgrounds, situations and experiences. Their stories involve both events of national importance and also intensely personal, family matters. Their reputations range from honourable to disreputable; their actions from successful to disastrous.

So what relevance do the stories of these women have for us today? First, we can learn how God really is interested in people (ordinary, sinful people) like us, and how He can use us to bring about His own perfect and loving plans. Among other things, they also teach us how (and how not) to respond to challenges such as temptation, doubt, fear, discouragement, intense longing, despair, and all the duties and demands of everyday life. Finally, we will discover that behind each woman stands the Lord Himself—always loving, always faithful, always in control, always working out His perfect plans, now revealed to us in Jesus Christ. By studying the lives of these women, not only can we learn practical lessons about how to live God's way in God's world, but we ourselves can come to know God, in Jesus Christ, for ourselves.

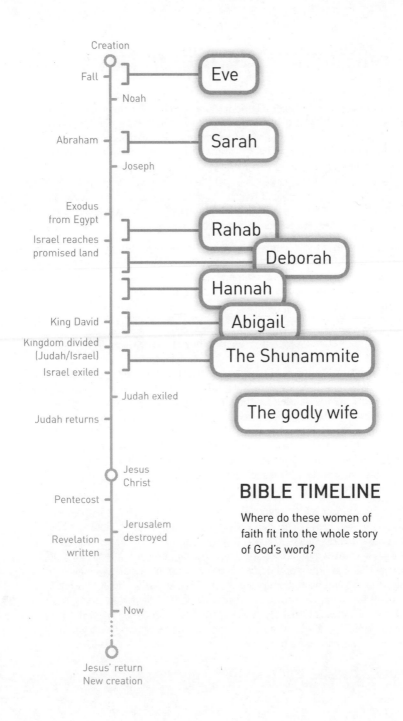

Creation

Fall

Noah

Eve

Abraham

Joseph

Sarah

Exodus
from Egypt

Israel reaches
promised land

Rahab

Deborah

Hannah

King David

Abigail

Kingdom divided
(Judah/Israel)

Israel exiled

The Shunammite

Judah exiled

Judah returns

The godly wife

Jesus
Christ

BIBLE TIMELINE

Pentecost

Jerusalem
destroyed

Revelation
written

Where do these women of
faith fit into the whole story
of God's word?

Now

Jesus' return
New creation

1

Genesis 3

EVE: FROM DOUBT TO DISASTER

⊕ talkabout

1. Share some experiences you have had of putting your trust in someone who let you down. What have you learned about who can be trusted?

⊕ investigate

2. To put our passage in context, look up the following key verses from Genesis 1 and 2 and write down a brief summary of each.

1 v 1

1 v 26

1 v 31

2 v 16-17

2 v 18

2 v 22-23

2 v 25

> Read Genesis 3

3. What tricks does the snake use to tempt Eve (v 1, 4-5)?

4. What does he want Eve to think God is like?

5. Look at how Eve responds to the snake. Why do you think she responds like this (v 2-3, 6)?

6. God had given a special role to Eve (2 v 18). In what way does she fail to carry it out (3 v 6)?

7. What do you think was at the heart of Adam and Eve's sin?

⊡ explore more

❯ Read Philippians 2 v 5-11

Compare the attitude of Jesus towards God with that of Adam and Eve. What strikes you about the differences?

⊡ apply

8. What bits of God's word do you find hardest to trust? Why?

• What should we be doing about this?

• What helps us to trust God more and how can we help one another?

⊡ getting personal

What impression of God might you be giving to those around you? That He's totally trustworthy, a God of goodness and love? Or something closer to the snake's picture of God?

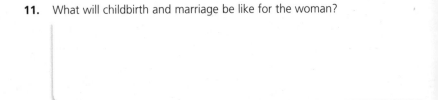

⊡ investigate

In the beginning, everything in God's creation was very good (1 v 31). All relationships were perfect and harmonious (between humans and God, between man and woman, between humans and the world) and everything was under God's rule. Now sin has entered the world and everything is spoiled.

9. Along with sin, what other terrible things have now become part of life in the garden?

10. What sentence does God pronounce on the snake (v 14-15)?

11. What will childbirth and marriage be like for the woman?

12. What will work be like for the man?

13. What signs of God's mercy can you see (v 20-24)?

⊡ explore more

How do both God's promise in Genesis 3 v 15, and God's action in 3 v 21, preview God's solution to the mess that human rebellion has caused (see Hebrews 2 v 14)?

⊟ apply

14. What have you learned about God from this study?

• Do you agree that not trusting God has terrible consequences? Why / why not?

• When Christians forget or ignore the consequences of not trusting God, what happens to holy living and evangelism?

• How can we help one another not to make this mistake (see Philippians 3 v 14-21, especially v 19b and 20)?

⬆ pray

Genesis 3 reminds us of how seriously God takes sin. Spend some time saying sorry to God for the ways in which you fail to trust him.

Thank God that, in the new creation, everything will be perfect again. You may like to **read Revelation 21 v 3-4** and turn the verses into a prayer of thanks and praise.

2 Genesis (various)
SARAH: FROM UNBELIEF TO GRACE

⊕ talkabout

1. What do you think most people in the street imagine a really great Christian to be like? What about you?

⊕ investigate

The first mention of Sarah (initially called Sarai) is in Genesis 11 v 29. She is Abraham's wife and she is barren. In this study, we will be looking at a number of different passages to discover more about Sarah's relationship with God. Try to find the main point(s) from each passage—and not to get side-tracked by any complicated bits!

▶ Read Genesis 15 v 1-5

2. What does God promise Abram?

▶ Read Genesis 16 v 1-6

3. What does this episode reveal about Sarah's attitudes…
   • to God?

• to Abraham?

• to Hagar?

optional

⊡ **explore more**

> **▶ Read Genesis 3**

In what ways were Sarah's attitudes and behaviour similar to Eve's?

➔ **apply**

4. In what areas of life are we most likely to take matters into our own hands, as Sarah did, instead of trusting God and leaving outcomes to Him? See Matthew 6 v 25-33; 1 Corinthians 7 v 17-28; 1 Corinthians 1 v 22-25.

• Can you add examples of your own?

Think carefully about your attitude to those areas of life which you find difficult to entrust to God. What should you learn from the consequences of Sarah's lack of trust? Are you in danger of storing up similar troubles for the future?

⊕ **investigate**

▶ **Read Genesis 17 v 1-8, 15-21**

5. Look carefully at what God says to Abraham. In what ways does God emphasise that He will keep His promises?

▶ **Read Genesis 18 v 1-15**

6. Why do you think Sarah laughs when she hears God's promise (v 10, 12)?

▶ **Read Genesis 21 v 1-7**

7. What do we learn about God from this passage?

❯ Read Genesis 21 v 8-10

8. What does this episode show us about Sarah's character?

❯ Read 1 Peter 3 v 5-6 and Hebrews 11 v 11-12

9. What positive qualities do these New Testament passages highlight?

10. From the passages you have read, how would you describe Sarah's character—both good and bad points?

11. Look back over the study. How would you describe the way in which God treats Sarah?

⤳ apply

12. In what ways does the story of Sarah's life encourage and challenge you?

• How should we respond when someone criticises the flaws and failures that they have come across in a Bible character or Christian?

⊡ getting personal

What impression of a Christian would someone (eg: parents, children, work colleagues) get from looking at your life? Someone who is "holier than thou" (and therefore must be a hypocrite)? Or a sinner just like them, but saved by God's wonderful grace?

13. Pick one aspect of God's character that has particularly struck you. What difference will it make to you this week?

⊡ pray

Spend some time thanking God for what you have learned about His faithfulness in keeping His promises, and His power to deliver those promises.

The Christian life involves trusting God's promises. Ask God to help you do that.

3 Joshua 2 and 6
RAHAB: FROM FEAR TO FAITH

⊕ talkabout

1. What do people think of when they hear the word "faith"? Discuss how you would you recognise whether someone has faith or not.

⊕ investigate

❯ Read Joshua 2

2. The people of Israel are on their journey to the promised land. How far have they got (see Joshua 1 v 1-3)?

3. Why is it surprising that God chooses to use someone like Rahab to help His people?

4. Summarise what happens in this chapter.

5. How much does Rahab understand about who God is? Look carefully at verses 9-11—what is her overwhelming emotion?

6. What is the deal that Rahab makes with the spies?

⤇ **apply**

7. What does this teach us about what God is like and the kind of people He uses?

- Think about Rahab's understanding of the LORD. Generally, how similar or different is the attitude of the non-Christians that you have come across?

- Why do you think our generation has lost its fear of almighty God?

• **Read Joshua 24 v 14; Psalm 34 v 9; Proverbs 1 v 7.** What does it mean for God's people to fear Him?

⊡ getting personal

Do you fear the LORD, or do you take His grace and forgiveness for granted?

Does fear of the LORD drive you to Him, or away from Him?

Do you understand how you can fear the LORD without being a slave to fear (see Romans 8 v 15)?

If you don't fear the LORD, or you fear Him wrongly, what should you do about it?

⊡ investigate

Having had a good report from the spies who went to Jericho (2 v 24), Joshua and the Israelites enter the land of Canaan. They cross the River Jordan, just as the Israelites crossed the Red Sea 40 years before (2 v 10).

⊡ explore more

This is a moment of great significance for the people of Israel— the battle against Jericho is not just another battle.

▶ **Read Genesis 17 v 1-8; 26 v 1-5; 28 v 10-15; Exodus 3 v 4-10; Joshua 1 v 1-6**

What does God promise? How do these passages expand your love for and understanding of the LORD?

▶ **Read Joshua 6 v 1-2, 15-25**

8. How do Rahab's actions demonstrate her faith?

9. Rahab is mentioned three times in the New Testament. Look at each in turn.

   a) **James 2 v 17, 24-26:** What does James say about faith? How is this true of Rahab?

   b) **Hebrews 11 v 1-2, 31:** Why does the author choose Rahab as a good example of saving faith?

   c) **Matthew 1 v 1, 5-6:** What is surprising and encouraging about seeing Rahab's name mentioned here?

☐ **apply**

10. Rahab put her faith into action. Sometimes we fail to do that. Can you think of specific examples?

   • You believe God is loving and in control: does your life show this or are you often anxious?

- You believe God answers prayer: how important is prayer in your life, and what difference does it make to your worries and longings?

- You believe that Christians have the promise of heaven: how much does your attitude (eg: to your possessions and home) reflect this?

- You believe God is loving, forgiving and merciful: how do you deal with your own failures and weaknesses?

⊡ getting personal

Look back over the study. What do you have to learn, in particular, from Rahab's attitudes and actions?

⬆ pray

In this session we have learned what it means to rightly fear the LORD (refer back to Question Seven). Praise God for what He has shown you about Himself.

Ask the Lord for the courage to put your faith into action—particularly in the areas you thought about in Question Ten.

The Christian life involves trusting God's promises. Ask God to help you do that.

4 Judges 4
DEBORAH: FROM OPPRESSION TO PRAISE

⊕ talkabout

1. Who is your hero? Share your ideas about what makes someone a hero.

⊡ investigate

God's people, the Israelites, are in the promised land—but they keep falling into evil ways. Each time, God hands them over to their enemies. Each time, they cry to Him for help. Each time, He sends them a rescuer—a "judge" who will lead them. Deborah is one of the judges God sends to help His people.

> **Read Judges 4**

2. There are a number of different people in this passage; explain briefly how each one fits into the story.

   • Ehud (see also 3 v 15)

   • Jabin

   • Sisera

   • Deborah

   • Barak

   • Heber

   • Jael

Israel keeps doing the same thing. Look at the passages below and answer the questions to spot the pattern that is repeated over and over again.

	3 v 7-11	3 v 12-15, 28-31	4 v 1-4, 23-24
What does Israel do?			
What does God do?			
How does Israel respond?			
What does God do now?			
What is the result?			

It is all summed up in 2 v 6-23. What is God like? What are the Israelites like?

3. What two dangers did the Israelites need rescuing from (4 v 3, 1)?

4. Why had the people of Israel turned to their evil ways again (4 v 1)? See also 2 v 16-19, especially v 19. What did their "faith" depend on?

5. How was Deborah different? For instance, how was she affected by Barak's weak and fearful response to God's message?

⊟ apply

6. What external influences (people, activities etc) might people today depend on to keep faithful to God?

• Compare the faith of someone who has been born again (John 3 v 3-8), with a person whose "faith" is only the result of external influences. What differences can you see?

⊡ getting personal

How well would you survive as a Christian if the external influences you've discussed were taken from you? If Christians around you acted fearfully and discouragingly, like Barak, could you stay faithful to serving Christ? How can you prepare yourself for situations like this?

⬇ investigate

7. What does God do about the Israelites' sin?

8. How does Deborah carry out her role as God's rescuer?

9. How does Deborah emphasise that God is the real hero, not herself or Barak (v 6-16, also v 23)?

⊡ explore more

optional

In Judges 4 Barak comes across as a bit of a wimp, but check out **Hebrews 11 v 32** for the New Testament verdict on him. See also Jesus' parable of two sons in **Matthew 21 v 32**.

What does God want and commend?
How can this encourage us when we struggle with trusting and obeying God?

10. What strikes you about Jael's actions (v 17-22)?

11. Go back over the passage. List all the things you have learned about God from this chapter.

12. In what ways is Jesus God's perfect rescuer? Try to think of some Bible verses that show this.

⊡ **explore more**

▶ **Read Judges 5**

What do we learn about God, and Deborah and Barak's understanding of him, from their song of praise?

↪ **apply**

13. Look back at your answer to Question Eleven. When you pray to God and talk to others about Him, do you downplay or miss out any aspects of His character? Why do you think that is?

• What do we need to do to make sure that this doesn't happen?

How well do you know the Bible's teaching about God? Do you understand why God must punish sin? Or how He can also forgive sinners? Have you been ignoring uncomfortable questions about God's character? What should you do about this?

↑ pray

No requests just yet—simply praise God for who He is and for sending Jesus, His perfect Rescuer.

Look back at Questions Six and Thirteen. Ask God to help you, and others you know, to respond rightly to the challenges highlighted in these questions.

5 1 Samuel 1
HANNAH: FROM GRIEF TO GRATITUDE

⟷ talkabout

1. Think of some difficult situations you have experienced. How do you tend to react? What is good (or not so good) about these reactions?

⤓ investigate

▶ Read 1 Samuel 1

2. From verses 1-8, describe the people in Hannah's family/marriage and the relationships between them.

3. Looking through verses 1-18, pick out the words and phrases the writer uses to describe Hannah's painful situation.

⋯ explore more

optional

▶ Read Genesis 11 v 30; 21 v 1-3; 25 v 21, 24-26; 29 v 31; 30 v 22; Judges 13 v 2-3, 24; Luke 1 v 7, 57-60

Who were the sons of these women? What part did they play in God's plans? What does this teach us about how God acts?

4. What do you find striking about the way in which Hannah responds to her situation (v 7-11)?

5. What does Hannah's prayer show us about her attitude to herself and to God (v 11-16)?

6. How does the writer convey Hannah's fervency in prayer? What do you understand by the phrase "pouring out her soul" (v 15)?

⊡ **apply**

7. If we are angry or upset about something, should we deal with it before we pray or in prayer?

• What can we learn about dealing with difficult circumstances from the following Bible prayers: Psalm 42 v 1-6 (depression); Psalm 51 (guilt); Psalm 55 v 1-9 (fear); Psalm 73 v 1-2, 16-28 (doubt); Psalm 102 v 1-14 and 24-28 (sickness)?

• Why do we slip into "shopping list" type prayers—rather than "pouring out our souls" to the Lord?

⊡ getting personal

Do the difficult situations considered in question one make you stay away from God or come to Him in prayer? What have you learned from Hannah's example?

⊡ investigate

8. Why do Hannah's feelings and attitude change (v 18)?

Israel was at a low point in its history. Although the Israelites were in the promised land, "everyone did as they saw fit" (Judges 21 v 25). It was important that they had a godly leader at this stage—and it was Samuel who would fulfil that role and lead the nation back to God.

9. What does God do for Hannah (v 19-20)?

10. How does Hannah show her obedience to God (v 21-28)? What is the motive for her obedience?

optional

⊡ explore more

> ❯ Read 1 Samuel 2 v 1-10

What do we learn about God's character from Hannah's song of praise?

⊟ apply

11. What other examples of sacrificial devotion to God, inspired by gratitude, have you come across? Why don't Christians act like this more often?

• How might people today criticise Hannah?

• Read **Mark 14 v 1-9** and **Mark 7 v 9-13**. What principles are given here?

• In what areas do we find it hard to give sacrificially back to God?

12. What have you learned about God, in relation to Israel and to Hannah? And what does that mean for us?

⬆ **pray**

As a group:

Thank God for what you have learned this session about His character and the way He deals with His people. Pray for each other, letting these characteristics shape your prayers.

On your own during the coming week:

Make some time to pour out your soul to the Lord. You may like to use these headings to direct your praying:

A doration—praise God for who He is

C onfession—say sorry for the ways you have let Him down

T hanksgiving—thank Him for the ways He has blessed you

S upplication—ask Him to act in situations that are on your heart

Remember in each case to "pour out your soul" to the Lord.

6 ABIGAIL: FROM FOLLY TO WISDOM

⟨↔⟩ talkabout

1. Talk about someone you know that you consider to be wise. Share and discuss your views on what makes someone truly wise.

⟨↓⟩ investigate

❯ Read 1 Samuel 25

Things aren't great for David at this point. His mentor, Samuel, has died (v 1). What's more, King Saul is trying to kill him (24 v 2; 26 v 2)—even though David twice spares Saul's life (24 v 11; 26 v 23). David is the Lord's anointed (1 Samuel 16 v 1, 12-13), which means that he will eventually become king. But for now, David is on the run.

2. Retell the story briefly in your own words.

3. Nabal and Abigail are very different characters. In what ways (v 2-3, 25, 33, 36)?

4. What does David ask for (v 4-8)?

5. Look at the way Nabal responds (v 10-11). What exactly makes him a fool?

6. Is David's reaction reasonable? Why/why not (v 12-13, 21-22)?

7. What qualities does Abigail show in what she does (v 14-23)?

8. How does she show good judgement in what she says to David (v 24-31)?

Abigail recognises that David is the LORD's anointed—in other words, that God has chosen him to be king. Look at what she says in verses 28 and 30. Of course, God's ultimate King is the Lord Jesus (see Philippians 2 v 9-11). So, just as Abigail acknowledged David as the LORD's anointed, we should acknowledge Jesus as the LORD's anointed and make Him our King.

⊡ explore more

❯ Read 2 Samuel 7 v 11-16 and Psalm 2

These words were originally spoken to or about David, the LORD's anointed.

In what ways do they also speak of Jesus and point to Him? See also Psalm 22.

How were these bitter experiences of David reflected in the life of Jesus?

Why did God's ultimate King need to suffer in this way?

→ apply

9. What lessons can we learn from the way that Abigail treated David, about how we need to approach God's greater King, the Lord Jesus Christ?

• How should this be reflected when we speak about Jesus to non-Christians, and explain what a Christian is?

• What does this teach us about true wisdom, and how different is this to the world's understanding of wisdom? (See 1 Corinthians 1 v 20-25; Colossians 2 v 2-3; 2 Timothy 3 v 15.)

⊡ getting personal

What will it mean for you to be wise—as Abigail was?

⊡ investigate

10. What does David praise God for (v 32-34, 39)?

11. How does the story end for David, Abigail and Nabal?

⊡ apply

12. Look at Abigail's achievements—a successful peacemaker who saved her household from disaster and kept David from serious sin. What qualities helped Abigail to achieve these things?

• Are these qualities characteristics that we either have or don't have—or can we develop them (see 2 Peter 1 v 3-9)? If so, how?

• What could have stopped Abigail from taking action to prevent David from sinning? What stops us from caring for one another in this way (see James 5 v 20)?

⊡ getting personal

Which of Abigail's qualities do you need to see more of in yourself? Think of one practical thing you can do to help yourself develop this.

⬆ pray

As a group:

- Think again about the parallels between the approach Abigail made to David and our approach to the Lord Jesus. What reasons are there for rejoicing and praising God?

- Pray for each other, that you would become increasingly wiser in what you say and do. (See James 1 v 5-8.)

On your own:

- If you are not sure that you have ever acknowledged Jesus as the LORD's anointed and made Him your King, why not do it today?
Here's a simple prayer:

Lord God, I'm **sorry** that I have lived my own way, rebelling against You.

Thank you that Your King, the Lord Jesus, died on the cross so that I can be forgiven.

Please come into my life by Your Holy Spirit and be my Lord and King. Amen.

7 2 Kings 4 v 8-37
THE SHUNAMMITE: FROM DEATH TO LIFE

⟷ talkabout

1. Do you know anyone who has come through a difficult situation? How would you judge that they had handled it well? What attitude to God would you look for?

⬇ investigate

Elisha is God's prophet, following in the footsteps of another prophet, Elijah. In this chapter of 2 Kings, God's people are in various hopeless situations and Elisha performs four miracles to help them. In the first miracle, he rescues a family from debt; in the third, he rescues some prophets from being poisoned; and, lastly, he miraculously supplies food for a hundred people. We will be concentrating on the second miracle (v 8-37).

▶ **Read 2 Kings 4 v 8-37**

2. What do verses 8-10 tell us about this woman's situation and her faith?

3. How does Elisha try to reward the woman and thank her for her kindness (v 11-16a)?

4. Look at the woman's answers to Elisha in verses 13b and 16b. In what way are they different? Why does she react as she does?

optional

⊡ explore more

There are a number of barren women in the Bible who receive a son from the Lord. In some cases, the son becomes a leader of God's people (eg: Joseph in Genesis 30 v 22, Samuel in 1 Samuel·1 v 20). In other cases, the birth ensures the continuation of God's people (eg: Isaac in Genesis 21 v 2-3, Jacob in Genesis 25 v 25-26).

This story is different again.

Why is this son given? What does this show about God's character?

⊡ apply

The woman was afraid to have her hopes of bearing a child raised, because she feared ultimate disappointment more than the sadness of her existing situation.

5. How do we show the same tendency eg: in our prayers, our relationships and our evangelism?

• What is the root cause of this kind of refusal to ask for God's help?

- What do we miss out on if we simply continue to put up with existing circumstances?

⬇ **investigate**

6. What qualities does the woman show in the way she deals with her son's illness and death (v 18-25a)?

7. In what ways does Elisha show sensitivity and understanding (v 25b-27)?

8. Re-read verses 27-28. What do you think the woman is feeling as she asks the question in verse 28?

9. How does this woman show faith?

10. What is the contrast in verses 29-37 between God and His servants, Gehazi and Elisha?

11. Look back over the passage. What changes have there been in the way the woman responds to God and His prophet (contrast verses 8-10 and 13b with verses 27-28, 30 and 37)?

12. What good things come out of the tragedy?

⊡ **explore more**

optional

Compare this story with that of the widow of Nain in **Luke 7 v 11-17**.

What similarities and differences do you notice?

The raising of the Shunammite woman's son is a preview of what Jesus would do several hundred years later.

And Jesus' miracle is a preview of what (see John 11 v 25)?

⤷ apply

13. How might this passage help someone who feels angry with God for the way things have turned out? In particular, what have you learned about...

• God's character and the way He works?

• faith? Do the woman's angry feelings show that she lacked faith?

• the reasons why God may allow us to suffer devastating experiences?

⊡ getting personal

What will help you to keep trusting God in situations like this? How can you pray for someone who is suffering right now?

⤒ pray

God gave the Shunammite woman a son. Praise Him for some of the good gifts He has given you. Praise Him most of all for the gift of eternal life in Christ Jesus.

Pray for anyone you know who is battling with tragedy and disappointment (perhaps yourself), that they would cling to God and keep trusting Him.

Proverbs 31 v 10-31

THE GODLY WIFE: FROM WISDOM TO HONOUR

8

⊕ talkabout

1. What qualities do you admire in women that you know? Make a list together of the qualities that are admired in our culture.

⊎ investigate

Each verse of this passage begins with a different letter of the Hebrew alphabet, using all 22 letters in order. Because of this arrangement, there is no obvious structure and the writer often jumps from one topic to another. One reason that poems were written like this was to make them easier to learn. It is known as an "acrostic" poem—like an "A to Z" of being a godly wife.

▶ **Read Proverbs 31 v 10-31**

2. Glance over the whole passage and make a list of the different people and activities this woman is involved with.

3. What is the evidence that this woman is a great wife and mother?

4. How does this compare with what the world tells us is important?

5. What is striking about the way she runs her business affairs?

6. How does she treat the poor?

⊡ **explore more**

optional

The book of Proverbs opens with "Wisdom" in the form of a woman (see 1 v 20 etc). It closes with this description of the ideal wife. Compare the ideal wife with the woman called "Wisdom" (see Proverbs 3 v 13-18, 4 v 5-9 and 9 v 1-6).

What similarities can you find?
Who is the teaching about wisdom for?
What about the teaching about the ideal wife?
Why do you think wisdom is "personified" like this in Proverbs? (See Matthew 11 v 19 and James 1 v 22-25—what do these passages show us about wisdom in the Bible?)

7. If beauty is "fleeting" (v 30), why do we find it so appealing?

8. Why is "a woman who fears the Lᴏʀᴅ" to be praised (v 30)?

⤷ apply

9. This passage is all about a married woman. What principles of wise living can you find that would be relevant to other people?

- What is the link between the "fear of the Lᴏʀᴅ" (v 30) and wisdom? See Proverbs 1 v 7; 2 v 1-6; 9 v 10; 15 v 33; Psalm 111 v 10; Job 28 v 28.

- How can we follow the instruction of Proverbs 4 v 7 to "get wisdom"?

⊡ getting personal

This woman was godly in her situation. What will it look like for you to be godly in yours?

Select one or two things about this godly woman that have particularly struck you. What practical steps can you take to make them part of your daily life?

⊡ explore more

optional

> **Read Colossians 2 v 2-3 and 1 Corinthians 1 v 30**

What does the New Testament add to our understanding of wisdom? Who is the ultimate ideal human (1 John 3 v 5)?

> **Read Romans 8 v 28-30 and 1 John 3 v 2-3**

Can Christians ever achieve the perfection represented by this ideal wife? How can these verses be an encouragement?

Does this woman seem a bit too good to be true? Isn't this just a religious version of the digitally-enhanced, cosmetically re-invented women that we see every day in magazines and on TV shows? Don't be depressed! This is the future you!—if you are a follower of Jesus Christ.

A real human—the Lord Jesus Christ—has already lived the good life of perfect wisdom that this ideal wife portrays. More than that, He came to take away our sins so that all those who put their trust in Him will become like Him (starting now—see 2 Corinthians 3 v 18) .

Now that we have seen what the good life of wisdom looks like in one particular everyday situation (the home), let this fantastic hope encourage you to be wise and godly in your situation!

10. Now that Jesus has come to our world and we live in the age of the gospel (we can know the good news about Jesus), what does it mean today to fear the LORD and live wisely (see Luke 12 v 5 and 2 Timothy 3 v 15)?

11. Read Galatians 6 v 9-10; 1 Corinthians 15 v 58; Colossians 3 v 16 and 1 Peter 3 v 15; 1 Thessalonians 5 v 1-11. How can a Christian put into practice the principles of wise living found in Proverbs 31?

12. **Read Titus 2 v 3-5.** What are the similarities with Proverbs 31? What motivates a Christian woman to live like this? (See also v 8 and 10.) In what way can our motives be sinful?

⊡ getting personal

What would it look like for you to live wisely as a Christian, not just as a woman? Pick one or two things that have particularly struck you. What practical steps can you take to make them part of your daily life?

⊡ pray

Think through things that you have learned in this session, for which you can praise and thank God. Are there things you need to confess as well?

In the light of the passage, pray for one or two women you know.

Wisdom isn't talked about—it's done! Ask God to help you put into practice what you have learned.

Women of Faith: Leader's Guide

INTRODUCTION

Leading a Bible study can be a bit like herding cats—everyone has a different idea of what the passage could be about, and a different line of enquiry that they want to pursue. But a good group leader is more than someone who just referees this kind of discussion. You will want to:

• correctly understand and handle the Bible passage. But also…

• encourage and train the people in your group to do this for themselves. Don't fall into the trap of spoon-feeding people by simply passing on the information in the Leader's Guide. Then…

• make sure that no Bible study is finished without everyone knowing how the passage is relevant for them. What changes do you all need to make in the light of the things you have been learning? And finally…

• encourage the group to turn all that has been learned and discussed into prayer.

Your Bible-study group is unique, and you are likely to know better than anyone the capabilities, backgrounds and circumstances of the people you are leading. That's why we've designed these guides with a number of optional features. If they're a quiet bunch, you might want to spend longer on talkabout. If your time is limited, you can choose to skip explore more, or get people to look at these questions at home. Can't get enough of Bible study? Well, some studies have optional extra homework projects. As leader, you can adapt and select the material to the needs of your particular group.

So what's in the Leader's Guide?
The main thing that this Leader's Guide will help you to do is to understand the major teaching points in the passage you are studying, and how to apply them. As well as guidance on the questions, the Leader's Guide for each session contains the following important sections:

THE BIG IDEA

One or two key sentences will give you the main point of the session. This is what you should be aiming to have fixed in people's minds as they leave the Bible study. And it's the point you need to head back towards when the discussion goes off at a tangent.

SUMMARY

An overview of the passage, including plenty of useful historical background information.

OPTIONAL EXTRA

Usually this is an introductory activity that ties in with the main theme of the Bible study, and is designed to "break the ice" at the beginning of a session. Or it may be a "homework project" that people can tackle during the week.

So let's take a look at the various different features of a Good Book Guide:

⊕ talkabout

Each session kicks off with a discussion question, based on the group's opinions or experiences. It's designed to get people talking and thinking in a general way about the main subject of the Bible study.

⬇ investigate

The first thing you and your group need to know is what the Bible passage is about, which is the purpose of these questions. But watch out—people may come up with answers based on their experiences or teaching they have heard in the past, without referring to the passage at all. It's amazing how often we can get through a Bible study without actually looking at the Bible! If you're stuck for an answer, the Leader's Guide contains guidance on questions. These are the answers to direct your group to. This information isn't meant to be read out to people—ideally, you want them to discover these answers from the Bible for themselves. Sometimes there are optional follow-up questions (see ☑ in guidance on questions) to help you help your group get to the answer.

⊡ explore more

These questions generally point people to other relevant parts of the Bible. They are useful for helping your group to see how the passage fits into the "big picture" of the whole Bible. These sections are OPTIONAL—only use them if you have time. Remember that it's better to finish in good time having really grasped one big thing from the passage, than to try and cram everything in.

➔ apply

We want to encourage you to spend more time working at application—too often, it is simply tacked on at the end. In the Good Book Guides, apply sections are mixed in with the investigate sections of the study. We hope that people will realise that application is not just an optional extra, but rather, the whole purpose of studying the

Bible. We do Bible study so that our lives can be changed by what we hear from God's word. If you skip the application, the Bible study hasn't achieved its purpose.

These questions draw out practical lessons that we can all learn from the Bible passage. You can review what has been learned so far, and think about practical differences that this should make in our churches and our lives. The group gets the opportunity to talk about what they personally have learned.

⊡ getting personal

These can be done at home, but it is well worth allowing a few moments of quiet reflection during the study for each person to think and pray about specific changes they need to make in their own lives. Why not have a time for reporting back at the beginning of the following session, so that everyone can be encouraged and challenged by one another to make application a priority?

⬆ pray

In Acts 4 v 25-30 the first Christians quoted Psalm 2 as they prayed in response to the persecution of the apostles by the Jewish religious leaders. Today however, it's not as common for Christians to base prayers on the truths of God's word as it once was. As a result, our prayers tend to be weak, superficial and self-centred rather than bold, visionary and God-centred.

The prayer section is based on what has been learned from the Bible passage. How different our prayer times would be if we were genuinely responding to what God has said to us through His word.

1 Genesis 3
EVE: FROM DOUBT TO DISASTER

THE BIG IDEA
Eve fails to trust and obey God's word—with terrible consequences.

SUMMARY
Eve is tempted by the devil to doubt God's goodness. As a result, she disobeys God's word and she leads her husband into sin also. The results are terrible and the perfect world they live in is ruined.

Note: It would be quite possible to spend a lifetime studying these wonderful, foundational chapters of Genesis. In a group Bible study, you will not have time to explore all the issues raised here (for example: where evil comes from; evolution and creation; whether Adam and Eve are real, historical people; etc). Try to concentrate on the main points and not get side-tracked. But take any questions seriously—make a note of them and deal with them on another occasion.

GUIDANCE ON QUESTIONS
1. Share some experiences you have had of putting your trust in someone who let you down. What have you learned about who can be trusted? The purpose of this question is to get people thinking about the issue of trustworthiness, and how we discern those who are untrustworthy, since it was Eve's culpable failure to trust in God's goodness, along with her unwarranted trust of the snake, that resulted in the disaster of human rebellion against God.

2. To put our passage in context, look up the following key verses from Genesis 1 and 2 and write down a brief summary of each [1 v 1, 26, 31; 2 v 16-17, 18, 22-23, 25]. The aim of this question is to put the passage into context and to look at the verses in chapters 1 and 2 that have a particular relevance for our study.

3. What tricks does the snake use to tempt Eve (v 1, 4-5)? The snake s identified as Satan (Revelation 12 v 9). His aim is to alienate mankind from God. He begins by encouraging the woman to question God. Note how he misquotes God's words in the process (compare 2 v 16-17 with 3 v 1). He goes on to deny God's word totally (v 4-5). His craftiness is shown in the way he includes bits of the truth (eg: their eyes were opened, they did know good and evil (v 5, 7, 22), along with the lies (contrary to the devil's assurance, they would die—v 4, 22, 5 v 5). Note that the devil is real—not a mythical character—and is still working to alienate us from God (1 Peter 5 v 8-9).

4. What does he want Eve to think God is like? He wants her to doubt God's goodness and love, and to think that God's commandment (2 v 16-17) was given out of selfishness, not love.

5. Look at how Eve responds to the snake. Why do you think she responds like this (v 2-3, 6)? When Eve replies to the serpent, she quotes God's words correctly but she exaggerates ("you must not *touch* it"). Note also how God's order in creation is reversed by Eve's actions. In creating the world, God established a particular order—

God in ultimate authority; then man and woman; then the animals (under man and woman's authority) (1 v 26). That order is now reversed as Eve does what the serpent says.

6. God had given a special role to Eve (2 v 18). In what way does she fail to carry it out (3 v 6)? In 2 v 18, Eve is designed to be Adam's helper—certainly not a derogatory term since it is used of God Himself in Psalm 33 v 20 as He "helps" Israel. In other words, Eve is designed to be the perfect companion for Adam and to work alongside him. Instead of this, Eve "helps" him into sin. Again, God's created order is reversed. For more on God's intended order, see Ephesians 5 v 21-33 and note how a husband is to lead lovingly and sacrificially (like Christ), and a wife is to entrust herself to that loving leadership. If this raises questions, you may want to discuss them further after the study itself.

7. What do you think was at the heart of Adam and Eve's sin? The essence of their sin was failing to trust God's word. They wanted to be like God and to take His place in deciding what is right and wrong. They rejected His authority over them. Note the difference between sin and sins. The heart of sin is rebelling against God (however politely). Sins are individual acts (like telling lies, thinking proud thoughts). Adam and Eve expressed their rebellion by eating the fruit they had been told not to eat. Traditionally it is thought to have been an apple—but there is actually no mention of the type of fruit.

EXPLORE MORE
Read Philippians 2 v 5-11. Compare the attitudes of Jesus towards God with that of Adam and Eve. What strikes you

about the differences? Christ humbled Himself and was exalted by the Father—in complete contrast to Adam and Eve. He did not, unlike Adam and Eve, consider equality with God something to be grasped.

8. APPLY: What bits of God's word do you find hardest to trust? Why? This will, of course, vary for each individual. For example—Romans 8 v 28 is sometimes hard to trust when life is tough; sometimes it is difficult to trust that heaven is a reality; we may find it hard to trust that God's teaching on certain issues is good (eg: homosexuality, singleness) etc.

- **What should we be doing about this?** Discuss the importance of… listening to God's word and living by faith, as opposed to being led by what we see and what looks desirable (3 v 6); understanding God's word accurately rather than going by what we think it says (3 v 3); identifying and listening to those who truly speak God's word, rather than those enemies of God, who have a different agenda; etc.

- **What helps us to trust God more and how can we help one another?** Answers may include: the importance of reminding each other of what God has done for us and testifying to His goodness; the example of those who have trusted God in difficult circumstances; the need for fellowship that allows Christians to come clean about these kinds of struggles and seek help; etc.

9. Along with sin, what other terrible things have now become part of life in the garden? Adam and Eve are now aware of evil, just as the devil promised—but it is a horrible anti-climax, not the rewarding experience they hoped for. Their relationship of innocence and ease with one other

(2 v 25) is replaced with shame (3 v 7). They vainly attempt to cover up their guilt with fig leaves (v 7). There is blame (v 12, 13), and enmity between humans and the animals (v 15). These things result in spoilt relationships—between God and humanity, between man and woman, between humanity and the animals. Ultimately, there is judgment (v 14-19), banishment and an end to unlimited access to God (v 24), and death (v 19b, 22).

Note: Verses 14-19 may raise a lot of questions. In answering Q9-11, try to look for the main points rather than getting lost in the detail. In each case, God's judgment strikes at the heart of each of the roles within creation. God had intended the various roles and relationships to be a blessing—but Adam and Eve chose to disobey and now they must suffer the consequences.

10. What sentence does God pronounce on the snake (v 14-15)? The snake is cursed and will crawl in the dust. There will be conflict between it and humans—when someone sees a snake they try to crush it; the snake tries to strike the person's heel.

11. What will childbirth and marriage be like for the woman? The woman's role of wife and mother will involve conflict and pain. "Desire" (v 16) probably means she will desire to have authority over her husband (the same word is used in Genesis 4 v 7), but he will try to dominate her. The judgment on the woman includes childbirth because giving birth to children is something that only a woman can do. But note that God intended a woman to be valued for herself alone—not just for her childbearing capacity (2 v 22-23). The main point is that her role will now be hard and her relationships spoilt.

12. What will work be like for the man? Work was a blessing (2 v 15)—now it is "painful toil" (3 v 17). All the time man will know that, in the end, he will return to dust. Look for the words that describe man and his work from now on—"cursed", "painful", "sweat", "dust". In v 17, "listened to" means "wrongly influenced by". Again, life is now hard work.

13. What signs of God's mercy can you see (v 20-24)? Continuation of life (v 20); God made garments for them (v 21); God saved them from an eternity of ruined relationships and toil (v 22-24).

EXPLORE MORE
How do both God's promise in Genesis 3 v 15, and God's action in 3 v 21, preview God's solution to the mess that human rebellion has caused (see Hebrews 2 v 14)? In the midst of all the doom and gloom of these verses, there is a glimmer of hope in verse 15. God promises that the snake will be crushed by the offspring of a woman. In Jesus' death on the cross, we see Satan's power completely destroyed. God's action in covering Adam and Eve's shameful nakedness requires the first recorded death of a living creature. But His action in removing human sin requires the death of His own Son.

14. APPLY: What have you learned about God from this study? For example, He is our Creator, our rightful Ruler. He is our generous Provider. He rules with righteousness, justice and grace. He hates sin and will not leave it unpunished. Despite our rebellion, He is still sovereign..

- **Do you agree that not trusting God has terrible consequences? Why / why not?** Sometimes it appears that people can get away with following their own wishes and not trusting God (eg: someone who decides to marry an unbeliever can appear blissfully happy). But ultimately, failing to trust God and live His way will have disastrous consequences, because those who do not know and trust Him will be separated from Him for ever.

• **When Christians forget or ignore the consequences of not trusting God, what happens to holy living and evangelism? Our holiness:** The hardships of the Christian life will begin to seem unattractive compared with the apparently care-free lives of non-Christians around us, and we will end up questioning whether it is worth trying to live God's way. **Our witness:** We will give up telling people about Jesus because, if there are no disastrous consequences of failing to trust God, there is no need to trust Him, and no need for Jesus to restore us to that relationship of trust in God.

• **How can we help one another not to make this mistake (see Philippians 3 v 14-21, especially v 19b and 20)?** We must encourage each other to keep our eyes on the future—on the Day of Judgment, the eternal destiny of those who do not believe in Jesus, and the eternal reward of those who love and serve Him in this world.

OPTIONAL EXTRA

Unless there is a crisis or specific need, Christians often don't find it easy to pray for one another—we don't know what to pray for? But the Bible contains many examples of great prayers that we can imitate. Why not take some time out later in the week to pray for yourself and others, using Bible passages to shape your prayers? For example, Ephesians 1 v 15-23 or 3 v 14-21; Philippians 1 v 3-11 etc. **Note:** Session 2 has a number of different passages. If you are studying as a group, you may like to ask members to try and read the verses before you meet up together.

Genesis (various)
SARAH: FROM UNBELIEF TO GRACE

THE BIG IDEA
Sarah is a mixture of godliness and ungodliness, faith and doubt—yet God graciously chooses to bless her.

SUMMARY
We look at the key events in Sarah's life and discover what kind of woman she is. Most of the Old Testament references show her in a less than favourable light, whereas the New Testament reveals more positive aspects of her character and life.

Throughout, the LORD is constant, showing Himself to be trustworthy and gracious, faithful and powerful. He blesses Sarah regardless of what she does/doesn't do.

Note: This study has more verses than usual to read. Keep an eye on the time! Try to get the main point from each passage and not get side-tracked by any complicated details! If people could make time to read the passages before meeting together to study them, it would help things tremendously! There is a reference to Sarah in Galatians 4. Although this is an important passage, it has not been included in this session as it does not contribute directly to our understanding of Sarah's character or her relationship with God. In Galatians, the experiences of Hagar and Sarah are used as an illustration or allegory. Ishmael is born as a result of human schemes and signifies those who try to secure salvation through their own efforts (ie: the Jews). Isaac, on the other hand, is born as a result of God's promise and signifies the way of the Spirit. See Genesis 16 for the OT background to this.

GUIDANCE ON QUESTIONS

Introductory paragraph: Their names are initially Abram (meaning "exalted father") and Sarai (meaning "princess"). God gives them new names in 17 v 5 and 15 (see question 5 for more on this).

1. What do you think most people in the street imagine a really great Christian to be like? What about you? Answers may reflect the views of those in the group, but it would also be worth considering the likely answer of the person in the street. Answers that only reflect positive aspects are fine; participants will become aware as the session progresses that this is not the whole picture.

2. What does God promise Abram [in Genesis 15 v 1-5]? This question sets the scene. The promises God makes to Abraham and Sarah are the backdrop to their entire lives. The key promise here is the one about a son—a son coming from Abraham's own body, ie: his biological son. God confirms His promise to Abraham by making a covenant with him (15 v 18).

3. What does this episode reveal about Sarah's attitudes…

- **to God?** Sarah finds it hard to live by God's promise and decides to take things into her own hands. She does not trust God to keep His promise or to work things out in His own time. She tries to secure an heir for Abraham through her servant-girl, Hagar. Although this form of surrogate motherhood was not unknown at the time, Sarah seems to realise that this is not the Lord's way— "perhaps I can build…"(16 v 2). There is also more than a hint of blame, resentment and impatience—"The Lord has kept me from having children". (Sarah's attitudes are similar to Eve's attitudes in Genesis 3—see Explore More below.)

- **to Abraham?** Sarah encourages Abraham to go along with her scheme. Abraham is passive and pliable and fails to exercise his headship role. He is guided by Sarah, not the Lord. Together, Abraham and Sarah fail to trust God. When relationships turn sour, Sarah blames Abraham (16 v 5).

- **to Hagar?** Sarah does not appear in a good light here either. She uses Hagar to achieve her own ends and when Hagar gets pregnant, we see the jealousy and hatred that is in Sarah's heart. Sarah ends up mistreating Hagar and driving her away.

EXPLORE MORE
Read Genesis 3. In what ways were Sarah's attitudes and behaviour similar to Eve's? In both cases, the women fail to trust God's goodness. The wife speaks (Genesis 16 v 2; 3 v 2); the husband listens and agrees to what the wife says, failing to exercise his headship role (16 v 2; 3 v 17); the wife takes someone/something and gives it to her husband (16 v 3; 3 v 6); the woman

blames (16 v 5; 3 v 13). Notice how the words in Genesis 16 are deliberately similar to those in Genesis 3.

4. APPLY: In what areas of life are we most likely to take matters into our own hands, as Sarah did, instead of trusting God and leaving outcomes to Him? See Matthew 6 v 25-33; 1 Cor 7 v 17-28; 1 Cor 1 v 22-25. Areas in which it is often difficult to trust that God's will and way are best probably include: money and financial security; relationships (especially for those who long to get married and/or have children); and evangelism that seeks to explain the Bible and the significance of the cross in our secular culture. These areas are reflected in the NT passages given, but there may be others that your group will highlight. Elicit and emphasise the consequences of Sarah's failure to wait for the Lord—the uncontrollable emotions that she suffered, the shame of her subsequent conduct towards Hagar and the longlasting bitterness that resulted between the two families.

• **Can you add examples of your own?** Encourage your group to discuss examples from their own lives, rather than examples from the lives of other people.

5. Look carefully at what God says to Abraham. In what ways does God emphasise that He will keep His promises? God confirms the covenant/ promises that He has already made (12 v 2-3; 15 v 1-21; 17 v 2). God's language underlines the certainty of the promise ("I will make… I will establish… I will give… I will bless…"). God also makes the promise very specific—the child will be Sarah's (17 v 16); the child is given a name (17 v 19); the promise will be fulfilled within a specified time-period (17 v 21). Humanly

speaking, it is impossible—Abraham will be 100 and Sarah will be 90 (17 v 17). But with God, nothing is impossible, as we shall discover (18 v 14). God gives both Abram and Sarai new names at this stage (17 v 5, 15)—Abraham ("exalted father of many") and Sarah (a newer form of the same word, "princess"). By giving Abram a new name, God was marking him in a special way as His servant. And He brings Sarah into the promise in her own right. Here are some extra questions which will help bring out the meaning:

⊻

• **Are God's promises new or have we heard them before?**
• **What words are repeated, as God speaks to Abraham, and what do they indicate?**
• **How much detail is given?**
• **What changes does God make, as a sign of His ownership of Abraham and Sarah and their future?**

6. Why do you think Sarah laughs when she hears God's promise (v 10, 12)? Up until now, the promises have been made to Abraham. Now Sarah's own faith is directly challenged. She laughs (18 v 12)—just as Abraham had at first (17 v 17). After all, she is infertile (11 v 30) and also past the age of child-bearing (18 v 11). The LORD rebukes Sarah for her laughter (18 v 14-15). His question in v 14 implies that she lacked trust. (Note that the LORD knows Sarah laughed, even though she is in the tent.) The three visitors are the LORD Himself (18 v 10, 13) and two angels (19 v 1).

7. What do we learn about God from this passage? Most importantly, the LORD keeps His promise. (Note the emphasis in

21 v 1-2: "as he had said … what he had promised"). Just as He said, a son, Isaac, is born to Abraham and Sarah. Despite Sarah's unbelief (18 v 9-15), God is gracious to her (21 v 1), bringing laughter and joy as He gives her a son (v 6).

8. What does this episode show us about Sarah's character? In 21 v 6-7, Sarah is full of joy and faith but here we see her hatred and intolerance. (Hagar and Sarah had fallen out 14 years before—see 16 v 6). Here, Isaac would have been about three years old and Ishmael was mocking him in some way. Sarah is factually right in what she says in 21 v 10—Ishmael would never share Isaac's inheritance. But this was because of God's choice (see 17 v 18-22; 21 v 12), not because of Sarah's decision to drive him out. Sarah's motives are not entirely spelled out—but her actions and words are, at the very least, harsh and unkind.

9. What positive qualities do these New Testament passages [1 Peter 3 v 5-6; Hebrews 11 v 11-12] highlight? These New Testament references are an important commentary on the Old Testament passages. Here we see Sarah's more positive qualities—and they must inform what we have learned about her from the Old Testament.
1 Peter 3 v 5-6: Sarah is especially highlighted as an example of someone who was submissive to her husband and did what he said (eg: Genesis 12 v 10-20; 20 v 1-18).
Hebrews 11 v 11-12: The commentators have different opinions on whether the faith commended here includes Sarah's or is just Abraham's. At the very least, Sarah is mentioned alongside these "heroes of faith" and many commentators believe she is singled out for special mention because of

her own faith in God.

10. From the passages you have read, how would you describe Sarah's character—both good and bad points? Like most of us, Sarah is a mixture of faith (Genesis 21 v 6; Hebrews 11 v 11-12) and doubt (Genesis 16 v 2-3; 18 v 12); godliness (1 Peter 3 v 6) and ungodliness (Gen 16 v 6; 18 v 15; 21 v 10).

11. Look back over the study. How would you describe the way in which God treats Sarah? Despite Sarah's unbelief and ungodliness at times, God is gracious and kind to her. He treats her according to His character—not according to what she deserves (Psalm 103 v 8-12). He is trustworthy, keeping His promises; He is powerful, giving a child to a woman who is barren and past childbearing age; and He is all-knowing, seeing everything in Sarah's heart.

12. APPLY: In what ways does the story of Sarah's life encourage and challenge you? Some possibilities: Don't give up when we fail because God doesn't give up on us; a reminder that ungodliness and unbelief have destructive consequences (eg: broken relationships).

- **How should we respond when someone criticises the flaws and failures that they have come across in a Bible character or Christian?** The Bible never hides the fact that even the greatest of men and women were sinners, and nor should we. Only when people understand that everyone is a sinner can they appreciate the grace of God in the way He has dealt with humans, the uniqueness of Jesus in His sinlessness, and their need of a Saviour.

13. APPLY: Pick one aspect of God's character that has particularly struck you. What difference will it make to you this week? Encourage group members to pick one aspect of God's character that has struck them and to be specific about what difference it will make.

OPTIONAL EXTRA

Have you ever tried meditating on a verse? Take, for example, Psalm 103 v 8. Read it through, slowly, a few times. Then read it again and think about each word in turn. Look at each word carefully; think about what it means; turn each word into a prayer. Give yourself plenty of time!

3 Joshua 2 and 6
RAHAB: FROM FEAR TO FAITH

THE BIG IDEA
Rahab is an example of someone who puts her faith into practice because she fears the LORD.

SUMMARY
The Israelites are on the verge of entering the promised land of Canaan after 40 years of wandering in the desert. Rahab protects the two Israelite spies sent by Joshua because she fears the God of the Israelites. Her faith is commended in the New Testament (Hebrews 11 v 31 and James 2 v 25) because it is saving faith that produces action. Although she knows little of God, Rahab shows by her actions where her faith is—and, in so doing, plays a part in God's salvation plan (Matthew 1 v 5; Joshua 6 v 16-17).

GUIDANCE ON QUESTIONS
1. What do people think of when they hear the word "faith"? Discuss how you would you recognise whether someone has faith or not. "Faith" is a greatly misunderstood word in our society. People popularly view it as one of the following: an intuitive sense that you either have or

don't have but can't acquire; a mystical force or energy; a harmless, even healthy, form of wishful thinking or delusion—believing something that can't be true. Most people believe that there is some merit in having faith, regardless of what you put your faith in! In the Bible, faith is the act of putting your trust or reliance in something/somebody. and it is always shown by the way you act. In the Bible, faith is recognised by its deeds (see questions 8-10 below). Here is an alternative question that some groups will enjoy (and some will not!)…

⊠

• **If you wanted to describe your faith as an animal, what animal would you choose and why?**

2. The people of Israel are on their journey to the promised land. How far have they got (see Joshua 1 v 1-3)? Moses had sent spies to explore the land 40 years earlier. Although they returned with a favourable report, the people rebelled and failed to enter the promised land (Numbers 13 – 14).

Moses is now dead and Joshua is leader. He sends two spies to check out the land before leading the Israelites to take possession of it.

3. Why is it surprising that God chooses to use someone like Rahab to help His people?

⌄

• If struggling: What is significant about Rahab's occupation and her nationality?

Rahab is described here in Joshua 2, and in the NT (Hebrews 11 v 31 and James 2 v 25), as a prostitute (although some translations try to rescue her reputation by adding "innkeeper" as a footnote!). She and her family were Canaanites—so she was a Gentile and, as such, not part of the people of God.

4. Summarise what happens in this chapter. You could ask members to do this individually and then share answers, or, to keep things shorter, you could ask someone to start, and then pass on to someone else to keep describing the outline of the events, and so on.

5. How much does Rahab understand about who God is? Look carefully at verses 9-11—what is her overwhelming emotion? Because Rahab is a Gentile, she has no Scriptures—she has heard her information on the grapevine. She recognises God's power. Notice the repetition of words/ideas in verses 9 and 11 ("fear ... hearts sank/melted ... courage failed" etc). She feared the Israelite people because she feared their God. For more on the drying up of the Red Sea, see Exodus 14 v 21-22; on the destruction of the Amorite

kings, see Numbers 21 v 21-35. (Also, Deuteronomy 2 v 24-25 prophesies that this will cause the nations to fear the Israelites.)

6. What is the deal that Rahab makes with the spies? Rahab asks for a "sure sign" (v 12)—the spies swear an oath (v 14) that they will spare her family. Some people have seen a link between the scarlet cord and the red blood of the cross/Passover. This is not something that is picked up in the NT and therefore there is no particular reason to think that the colour of the cord is very significant.

7. APPLY: What does this teach us about what God is like and the kind of people He uses? People are likely to focus their answers on the second part of the question, perhaps highlighting the fact that Rahab was both a foreigner and a prostitute, as discussed in Q3. Neither of these are commendable as a reason for God's choice (although this does show that God sovereignly chooses people who are very different from our ideas about who would be most suitable). Revisit Q5 to direct your group to the importance of fearing the LORD. Rahab's fear drives her to throw herself on the mercy of this all-powerful God that she has heard of. This shows us that God must be recognised for who He is—the sovereign, all-powerful King of the universe, who can never permit resistance and rebellion against His rule. It also shows us that the people He chooses to use are those who fear Him.

• Think about Rahab's understanding of the Lord. Generally, how similar or different is the attitude of the non-Christians that you have come across? It is likely that your group's experience will lead them to conclude that mostly people today do not fear the LORD.

- **Why do you think our generation has lost its fear of almighty God?** As well as prevailing cultural trends like anti-authoritarianism and increasing secularism, it may be that Christians themselves fail to show fear of the LORD in the way they live their lives, and downplay parts of the Bible that command us to fear the LORD (see passages below).

- **Read Joshua 24 v 14; Psalm 34 v 9; Proverbs 1 v 7. What does it mean for God's people to fear Him?** The Bible passages referred to are all instructions to fear the LORD, given to God's people. This doesn't mean that we should run away from God. Rather, as shown by Rahab's example, in understanding that God is the sovereign King of the universe, who is utterly displeased at the way we have lived our lives, and in fear of what His anger will mean for us, we should turn to God and throw ourselves on His mercy.

EXPLORE MORE
Read Genesis 17 v 1-8; 26 v 1-5; 28 v 10-15; Exodus 3 v 4-10; Joshua 1 v 1-6 What does God promise? How do these passages expand your love for and understanding of the Lord? If numbers allow, it might be worth dividing the group into five sub-groups and asking each to look up one reference and then report back to the rest of the group. The references describe God's covenant with Abraham, Isaac and Jacob, and His promise to Moses and Joshua to bring them into the promised land. Our God keeps His promises and is faithful over generations. Can He not be trusted with both the big decisions and the small details of our lives too?

8. How do Rahab's actions demonstrate her faith? Her faith is not simply "head knowledge", recognising something to be true but doing nothing about it. She fears God and she acts on her faith, putting her own life in danger by deceiving the king's men and making a deal with the Israelite spies.

9. Rahab is mentioned three times in the New Testament. Look at each in turn.
a) James 2 v 17, 24-26: What does James say about faith? Real, saving faith always results in action. There is no disagreement between Paul and James. They both talk about faith and deeds. Paul focuses on faith as opposed to deeds. He emphasises that we are saved by faith alone and that we cannot justify ourselves before God by what we do (Romans 3 v 28). James focuses on true faith as opposed to dead faith, seeing deeds as evidence of real, saving faith. True saving faith will always be accompanied by good deeds. Faith that is just "head knowledge", without action, is not really faith at all (James 2 v 17). John Calvin said: "We are saved by faith alone, but saving faith is never alone". Ephesians 2 v 8-10 says: "For it is by grace you have been saved, through faith … created in Christ Jesus to do good works". **How is this true of Rahab?** Rahab acted on what she knew of God—and so demonstrated that her faith was genuine, saving faith.

b) Hebrews 11 v 1-2, 31: Why does the author choose Rahab as a good example of saving faith? Hebrews focuses on those who demonstrated their faith by trusting God even when the outcome could not be seen. Again, it is not Rahab's words to the spies, but her actions on their behalf that qualify her for a place alongside Abraham and other heroes of faith.

c) Matthew 1 v 1, 5-6: What is surprising and encouraging about seeing Rahab's name mentioned here? A foreign, pagan prostitute not only plays a crucial part in bringing God's people into the promised land, but also has the privilege of being in the family line of Christ.

10. APPLY: Rahab put her faith into action. Sometimes we fail to do that. Can you think of specific examples?
- **You believe God is loving and in control: does your life show this or are you often anxious?**
- **You believe God answers prayer: how important is prayer in your life, and what difference does it make to your worries and longings?**
- **You believe that Christians have the promise of heaven: how much does your attitude (eg: to your possessions and home) reflect this?**
- **You believe God is loving, forgiving and merciful: how do you deal with your own failures and weaknesses?**

Encourage the group to be specific in their application. If they don't come up with examples of their own, move on to discuss the examples given. It may be good to split into pairs to answer these questions and then report back, so that members can talk more freely/personally. (There will, of course, be many other areas of the Christian life on which you could focus.)

OPTIONAL EXTRA

Why not have a go at writing a spiritual journal? Many Christians throughout history have done this and found it very helpful. You can use it to record lessons learned (what a fantastic aid for remembering what was taught last Sunday in church, or the main points of last session in this Women of Faith course!), blessings received, prayers answered, questions (your own or those that you were asked and couldn't answer), challenges that you need to address, action that you should take and changes to be made. You needn't write pages, nor write every day. It could become part of your personal Bible-reading time or whatever works for you, but don't forget to regularly review what has been written—for your own encouragement, challenge and prayer.

4 DEBORAH: FROM OPPRESSION TO PRAISE

THE BIG IDEA

God rescues the Israelites through Deborah. She serves God's people faithfully and leads them out of oppression into a time of peace and strength.

SUMMARY

The real hero of this episode is God Himself. His people are fickle and do evil—again and again (Judges 3 v 7, 12; 4 v 1). So God hands them over to their enemies. They cry out for help and God saves them by sending a rescuer. Deborah is the fourth judge sent to rescue the Israelites (after Othniel, Ehud and Shamgar). Time and again, the Israelites are faithless. Time and again, God is patient and merciful.

GUIDANCE ON QUESTIONS

1. Who is your hero? Share your ideas about what makes someone a hero. A question to pave the way for Q9.

2. There are a number of different people in this passage; explain briefly how each one fits into the story.
- **Ehud (see also 3 v 15):** the judge who has just died (3 v 15; 4 v 1)
- **Jabin:** a Canaanite king (4 v 2)
- **Sisera:** the commander of Jabin's army (4 v 2)
- **Deborah:** a prophetess who was judge of Israel (4 v 4-5)
- **Barak:** son of Abinoam, a soldier in Deborah's army (4 v 6)
- **Heber:** a Kenite who had left his tribe and moved north, an ally of Jabin (4 v 11, 17)

- **Jael:** wife of Heber, the one who killed Sisera (4 v 17, 21)

EXPLORE MORE

Israel keeps doing the same thing. Look at the passages below [in the table on p26] and answer the questions to spot the pattern that is repeated over and over again. The Israelites do evil in God's sight. So God is angry and hands them over to their enemies. The Israelites cry out to Him for help. God has mercy on them and sends them a judge. Once again there is peace and strength. But when the judge dies, the Israelites again do evil in God's sight and so the pattern repeats itself. **It is all summed up in 2 v 6-23. What is God like? What are the Israelites like?** God is consistently merciful and faithful—but the Israelites are consistently fickle and faithless.

3. What two dangers did the Israelites need rescuing from (4 v 3, 1)? The Israelites were facing two sorts of danger:
a) Physical danger—from Sisera's cruel oppression.
b) Spiritual danger—once again, they had fallen into sinful ways.

4. Why had the people of Israel turned to their evil ways again (4 v 1)? See also 2 v 16-19, especially v 19. What did their "faith" depend on? While a judge was alive, the people were faithful to God—but as soon as the judge died, they showed their true character and returned to their evil ways. "Evil ways" means worshipping Baal (2 v 11) ie: worshipping other gods, not the true God. It seems that it was only external influences that were keeping them faithful to God because they failed to continue trusting Him when the judges were gone.

5. How was Deborah different? For instance, how was she affected by Barak's weak and fearful response to God's message? If Deborah's faith had depended on external influences, the godlessness of the Israelites and the overwhelming strength of the enemy (4 v 3) alone would have made her think twice. But in addition, her message from God did not get the enthusiastic reception that she might have expected from her chosen commander. Barak's response (4 v 8) seems grudging, fearful and designed to ensure that responsibility for any resulting disaster would rest squarely on Deborah. Imagine the courage and faith in God required for a woman to lead an army to battle. Clearly from her response (4 v 9), Deborah is disappointed with Barak, but she never wavers in her determination to see God's promise fulfilled.

6. APPLY: What external influences (people, activities etc) might people today depend on to keep faithful to God? Give your group time to think how the fact of the Israelites' "faith" based on external influences may also be relevant to us. Is it only people/activities that stop us from giving up our faith (eg: a particular Christian friend, or going to church weekly)? Note that the NT does place great importance on meeting together and encouraging one another, but this is not what produces faith—rather, this is the fruit that faith produces (see Heb 10 v 19-25).

• **Compare the faith of someone who has been born again (John 3 v 3-8), with a person whose "faith" is only**

the result of external influences. What differences can you see? There may be people in the group who would benefit from discussing the need for new birth through God's Holy Spirit (John 3 v 3). There are many distinguishing marks of someone who has been born again, absent in someone who hasn't been born again—eg: trust of God in difficult times; perseverance and faithfulness; sorrow and repentance for their own sin and failure; serving God's people rather than simply receiving from God's people; love for Christ and His people; submission to God's word; a desire to tell others about Jesus; prayer etc.

7. What does God do about the Israelites' sin? God is deeply angered by the Israelites' sin. He will not tolerate it and He actively hands them over to their enemies—as He has done on previous occasions. This shows us how seriously He takes sin. But He is also compassionate—He hears the Israelites' cries and saves them through Deborah. It doesn't actually say that God "raised her up", as recorded about some of the other rescuers (eg: 3 v 9, 15), but God certainly uses Deborah to save His people.

8. How does Deborah carry out her role as God's rescuer? Deborah leads the people out of oppression into a time of peace and prosperity. She is a prophetess and speaks God's words to them—not publicly, it seems, but privately to individuals, under the "Palm of Deborah". She settles their disputes and brings God's commands to them. She does not seem to have a military role in the way that other male judges had—she hands this over to Barak. She serves God's people by relying on God and bringing the Israelites out of their evil

ways, back into dependence on Him.
Note: Some people use this passage to argue for female leadership in the church. Although this is an important issue, it is beyond the scope of this study to deal with it here. Try not to get side-tracked but concentrate on what the text actually says, and aim to deal with any other points after the main study. For a detailed treatment of this subject, see *Recovering Biblical Manhood & Womanhood* by John Piper & Wayne Grudem.

9. How does Deborah emphasise that God is the real hero, not herself or Barak (v 6-16, also v 23)? Look particularly at v 6, 7, 9, 14, 15 and 23. The rescue is at God's initiative and in God's strength. He promises it—He achieves it. Make sure that the meaning of v 7 is clear. (Ask, for example: Who is the "I" in v 7?) The "I" is God—Deborah is reporting His words (see v 6). In other words, it is God who will lure Sisera and give him into Barak's hands. (The "woman" in v 9 is not identified, but is undoubtedly Jael.)

EXPLORE MORE
[In Hebrews 11 v 32 and Matthew 21 v 32], what does God want and commend? How can this encourage us when we struggle with trusting and obeying God? Despite Barak's disappointing initial response to Deborah, he is commended by God as one of the "heroes of faith" in Hebrews 11 v 32. This is because he did end up doing what Deborah had told him to. What God wants from us is our obedience—He sees and commends our final obedience to Him, rather than our weak and wobbly first response to His word. Similarly, Jesus' parable of the two sons shows that God is not impressed (or otherwise) by how we start out. Rather,

what's important is how we end up—trusting and obeying Him, not ignoring or rejecting Him.

10. What strikes you about Jael's actions (v 17-22)? Jael is quick-witted; she makes the most of the opportunity she has; she is fearless and daring. Sometimes people comment that it is Jael's treacherous actions that bring about the victory over Sisera. She ignores the treaty between Jabin and Heber (v 17), flouts the accepted codes of hospitality and betrays Sisera's trust. Whatever we may feel about what she does, God certainly uses her to save His people from Sisera—a cruel man who was oppressing His people (4 v 3) and probably raping captive Israelite girls (5 v 30).

11. Go back over the passage. List all the things you have learned about God from this chapter. For example, God acts to save His people. He is patient, merciful, compassionate and faithful (even though Israel are faithless). He does not give up on them. He is powerful and mighty. He is a warrior who fights for His people and destroys His enemies. He hates sin; it provokes Him to anger and He acts accordingly. We should not be embarrassed at God's power and His destruction of evil. He is not a meek and mild, soft and gentle wimp, willing to be pushed around and ignored.

12. In what ways is Jesus God's perfect rescuer? Try to think of some Bible verses that show this. You could spend a whole study on this! Think about how Jesus is the ultimate rescuer sent by God. For example, Jesus brings salvation (1 John 4 v 14); He comes to serve God's people and to give His life for them (Matthew 20 v 28); He doesn't just bring, but is, God's word to us (John 1 v 14); He reveals God to us (John 14 v 9); He shows us how to live God's way (1 Peter 2 v 21-22); He defeats God's enemies (Colossians 2 v 15); He leads God's people into perfect peace (John 14 v 1-3; Revelation 21 v 3-4)—to mention but a few! Don't feel you need to cover all of these—maybe suggest one aspect each. There will be an opportunity to praise God for these wonderful truths in prayer at the end of the session.

EXPLORE MORE
Read Judges 5. What do we learn about God, and Deborah and Barak's understanding of Him, from their song of praise? Judges 5 is a celebration of God's victory, a song praising God for His deliverance. Read through the chapter and spot which of God's actions and characteristics are highlighted.

13. APPLY: Look back at your answer to Q11. When you pray to God and talk to others about Him, do you downplay or miss out any aspects of His character? Why do you think that is? There may be a tendency to focus either on God's love or His judgment. Reasons for this include: personality—warm fuzzy people are attracted by God's grace and repelled by His judgment, whereas hard, rigorous personalities may be more attracted by teachings about God's sovereignty, holiness and judgment, as are religious people who seek to earn God's approval, and feel uncomfortable with the idea of grace; culture—the free-and-easy western culture of today wants a God who is relaxed about moral issues and always forgiving, whereas historically, the idea of a God who judges, even avenges, was prevalent; theological understanding—if we have read or heard only selected parts of the Bible we

will only have a partial understanding (in fact, a misunderstanding) about God. But underlying all of these, the ultimate reason that we must face up to is our sin, which refuses to accept God as He has revealed Himself to us.

- **What do we need to do to make sure that this doesn't happen?** We must be faithful to God's word and speak about both His love and His hatred of sin. We need to constantly read the whole word of God and our churches need to teach all of it.

OPTIONAL EXTRA
Times of discouragement, suffering, and opposition will come to every Christian, so it's worth preparing ourselves for situations like these, before we are in the thick of it. Here are some things that can help a Christian to stand firm in times of trouble: developing a routine of personal Bible-reading and prayer that can keep you going when facing difficulties; memorising key passages of Scripture that you can bring to mind at moments of stress or crisis (eg: Psalm 23, Romans 8 v 28-39 etc.); developing friendships with mature Christians who will pray with you and look out for you (see optional extra for Session 5); reading about Christians who have suffered, and being inspired by their perseverance and achievements (eg: *My Heart in His Hands* by Sharon James—a biography of Ann Judson, missionary to Burma). Why not choose one of these practical steps and start putting it into action this week?

5 1 Samuel 1
HANNAH: FROM GRIEF TO GRATITUDE

THE BIG IDEA
Hannah is a godly woman in great pain, who prays fervently and trustingly to the Lord.

SUMMARY
Hannah is the first, much loved, barren wife of Elkanah. She appears in Israel's history as the mother of Israel's last and greatest judge, Samuel (after which Israel is ruled by a succession of kings). Hannah is one of a number of barren women who are eventually given a child by the LORD, and whose son plays an important role in Israel's history (eg: Sarah, Rebekah, Rachel). Bearing in mind this context, we will be focusing on Hannah's fervent, trusting prayer.

GUIDANCE ON QUESTIONS
1. Think of some difficult situations you have experienced. How do you tend to react? What is good (or not so good) about these reactions? Think about what we tend to do (eg: Do we rush to friends/family for comfort or do we pray?) and about our attitudes (eg: Do we tend to be bitter/resentful or do difficult situations lead to a new dependence on God and humility?). Perhaps ask group members to think about a specific situation they have been in (without necessarily sharing all the details).

2. From verses 1-8, describe the people in Hannah's family/marriage and the relationships between them. Look at what we know about each individual, and then at the relationships between them. Identify the positives as well as the

negatives about Hannah's situation eg: Hannah was much loved by Elkanah (v 5, 8). Elkanah's genealogy shows that he was probably a wealthy man. He may have taken a second wife because of Hannah's infertility. Although monogamy was God's design (Genesis 2 v 23-24) and the norm in the Old Testament, there is evidence of polygamy (Genesis 4 v 19; Deuteronomy 21 v 15-17). Their practice of worship/sacrifice (v 4 probably refers to a family festival) shows that they were godly folk. There was a temple/tabernacle at Shiloh—not the great temple in Jerusalem (which hadn't yet been built), but still a permanent structure of some description (it had doorposts, v 9).

3. Looking through verses 1-18, pick out the words and phrases the writer uses to describe Hannah's painful situation. Especially v 6, 7, 8, 10, 11, 15, 16, 18. Although it was the LORD who closed Hannah's womb, there is no indication that it was a judgment on Hannah.

EXPLORE MORE
Read Genesis 11 v 30; 21 v 1-3; 25 v 21, 24-26; 29 v 31; 30 v 22; Judges 13 v 2-3, 24; Luke 1 v 7, 57-60. Who were the sons of these women? Genesis 11 and 21— Sarah, mother of Isaac; Genesis 25— Rebekah, mother of Jacob; Genesis 29 and 30—Rachel, mother of Joseph; Judges 13— wife of Manoah, mother of Samson; Luke 1—Elizabeth, mother of John the Baptist. **What part did they play in God's plans? What does this teach us about how God acts?** The mother's initial infertility serves to underline the importance of the child who is

to be born and the fact that he is God's gift. Clearly, God does not always choose to answer the prayers of barren women in this way.

4. What do you find striking about the way in which Hannah responds to her situation (v 7-11)? You could highlight Hannah's patience (v 7); the way she expressed her emotions; her fervency and her lack of bitterness in prayer; the lack of selfishness in her request; her desire to serve God; etc. Giving up one's child in this way is hard for us to understand. By making this vow, Hannah was recognising that any son she might have would be in answer to prayer— so she vowed to give him back to God. The reference to the razor (v 11) implies that Samuel would be a Nazirite (like Samson—see Judges 13 v 3-5, also Numbers 6 v 1-8). The uncut hair was a sign of consecration to the LORD. To Hannah, this was an appropriate way of showing her gratitude.

5. What does Hannah's prayer show us about her attitude to herself and to God (v 11-16)?

⌄

• **How does she address God and what does this title mean?**

Look at how she addresses God and how she describes herself in relation to Him. She recognises her inability to change her situation—and God's ability to act. "LORD of hosts" (RSV, ESV) or "LORD Almighty" (NIV)—the "hosts" were armies belonging to the LORD, sometimes armies of angels (Joshua 5 v 14) or men (1 Samuel 17 v 45). The name "LORD of hosts" therefore indicates God's infinite power and resources.

6. How does the writer convey Hannah's fervency in prayer? What do you understand by the phrase "pouring out her soul" (v 15)? Her weeping (v 10), her vow (v 11), her persistence (v 12), "pouring out her soul" (v 15), her anguish and grief (v 16), etc. On "pouring out", see Psalm 62 v 8.

7. APPLY: If we are angry or upset about something, should we deal with it before we pray or in prayer? The prayers from Psalms referred to below suggest that it is in prayer that we are best able to deal with difficult issues. Some mistakenly believe that they cannot come to God when they are feeling upset or angry, and this has the disastrous effect of keeping them away from the One who alone can comfort and guide us with true wisdom. Dealing with difficult issues in prayer makes us reflect on God's view of these things—His promises, purposes and character. Otherwise, we run the risk of drifting into worldly ways of thinking and coping.

• **What can we learn about dealing with difficult circumstances from the following Bible prayers: Psalm 42 v 1-6 (depression); Psalm 51 (guilt); Psalm 55 v 1-9 (fear); Psalm 73 v 1-2, 16-28 (doubt); Psalm 102 v 1-14 and 24-28 (sickness)?** If possible, divide the group into twos or threes, each looking at one psalm.

• **Why do we slip into "shopping list" type prayers—rather than "pouring out our souls" to the Lord?** Discuss the following: Does the group agree that this can be a problem—if not, in what other ways can we learn from Hannah? Why are "shopping list" prayers a problem ie: what does this say about the quality of relationship that we have with God? Share ideas on how to avoid this: remember the relationship at the heart of prayer—we pray to our heavenly Father (eg: Matthew 6 v 5-15); remember His character—don't forget His willingness to answer (because of His love) and ability to answer (because of His power); practical suggestions—making enough time to pray, using our "best" time to pray etc.

8. Why do Hannah's feelings and attitude change (v 18)? Hannah's circumstances remain the same. But because she takes Eli at his word and puts her trust in the God of Israel, she is now full of joy and confidence.

9. What does God do for Hannah (v 19-20)? V 19—"remembered" (also in v 11) does not mean that God had a faulty memory before this, but is an indication that He is about to carry out His purposes.

10. How does Hannah show her obedience to God (v 21-28)? What is the motive for her obedience? She faithfully carries out her vow—years after she prayed. (Babies were usually nursed for two to three years.) The translation of Elkanah's first words in verse 23 is slightly unclear. It probably means: "May the LORD enable you to fulfil your vow". A three-year-old bull was more than required for a sacrifice and, as such, it was a mark of their gratitude.

EXPLORE MORE
Read 1 Samuel 2 v 1-10. What do we learn about God's character from Hannah's song of praise? There is no one like God; He knows everything (v 1-3); He raises the lowly and brings down the powerful; He is Creator of the world (v 4-8); as Judge, He guarantees the safety of those who love Him and the fall of those

who oppose Him (v 9-10). This song may have been an existing hymn or song of early Israel, which Hannah made her own.

11. APPLY: What other examples of sacrificial devotion to God, inspired by gratitude, have you come across? Why don't Christians act like this more often? This question is an opportunity for people in the group to be encouraged in grateful, sacrificial living by the experiences of others. Christians may lose gratitude because… we allow ourselves and our hardships to dominate our thinking; we forget what it was like to be a non-Christian; we don't regularly count our blessings; in our rich society we have drifted from putting our dependence in God; we don't really pray and so we do not see prayers answered etc.

• **How might people today criticise Hannah?** For relinquishing her parental responsibility, or for putting fulfilment of a promise before "the best interests of her child". People may question whether Hannah really loved Samuel if she was able to give him up like this, not understanding that the reason Hannah could act in this way was because she trusted a God of mercy, generosity and power, and was confident that He would look after the son He had given her.

• **Read Mark 14 v 1-9 and Mark 7 v 9-13. What principles are given here?** 14 v 1-9 shows that costly and sacrificial devotion to the Lord is not wasted, but is commended by Him. However, Mark 7 v 9-13 warns against using the pretext of serving God as an excuse for neglect of our duty to care for those who depend on us.

• **In what areas do we find it hard to give sacrificially back to God?** Allow people to speak personally, but here are a couple of suggested areas. Standard of living—how many Christians are prepared to downsize to release funds for gospel work or to reach people outside middle-class, Bible-belt areas? Children's education and career—how often are Christian parents one of the greatest obstacles to young peoples' involvement in Christian activities while at college, or their sacrifice of a "proper" career in order to become a minister or missionary?

12. APPLY: What have you learned about God, in relation to Israel and to Hannah? And what does that mean for us? *Israel:* Although things were bad for Israel (Judges 21 v 25), God was still in control; He carried out His purposes and provided the godly leader that Israel needed. *Hannah:* Her desperate situation was not too big for God to handle. And His overall purposes were far greater than she could ever have imagined.

Ourselves: Think of our own difficult situations (Q1). They are not too hard for God to handle. He may not answer in the way we expect or want, but He is loving and powerful and in control.

OPTIONAL EXTRA

This may be a good opportunity to discuss the benefits of prayer triplets—ie: meeting with a couple of other Christians on a regular basis (eg: weekly or fortnightly) to pray together. They can be a great way to learn to pray, to keep praying for non-Christian friends, to bring difficult situations to the Lord, and to support one another in the Christian life. Don't just talk about it—do it!

---

6 1 Samuel 25
ABIGAIL: FROM FOLLY TO WISDOM

THE BIG IDEA
Abigail shows her wisdom—in contrast to her husband Nabal, whose name is "fool".

SUMMARY
This chapter tells of a confrontation between David, who will one day be king, and Nabal, a rich but foolish and harsh farmer. David asks Nabal for provisions for his men but Nabal rudely refuses him. Abigail acts wisely and prevents David from sinning by her swift action and eloquent words.

Note: David has been marked out as the future king by the Lord Himself (1 Samuel 16 v 1,12-13)—a fact also recognised by the current king, Saul (1 Samuel 24 v 20).

GUIDANCE ON QUESTIONS
1. Talk about someone you know that you consider to be wise. Share and discuss your views on what makes someone truly wise. Encourage the group to say what they really think about this discussion question, rather than making them give the "right" answer.

2. Retell the story briefly in your own words. See summary section above.

3. Nabal and Abigail are very different characters. In what ways (v 2-3, 25, 33, 36)? Nabal and Abigail are a complete contrast—folly and wisdom—and this is one of the keys to the passage. Nabal means "fool" in Hebrew (v 25). Though he's rich, he is mean, surly and evil in his actions. Even his wife thinks he is a good-for-nothing (v 25). (He is a Calebite, ie: a descendant of Joshua's companion, Caleb). Abigail is his opposite—wise, beautiful and intelligent.

4. What does David ask for (v 4-8)?
(There is no other reference to David having looked after Nabal's men in the OT; the only details we have are in this chapter.) David sends his greetings (note the humility of "your son", v 8). He is effectively asking for payment for the protection he gave to Nabal's shepherds. This was not an unreasonable request, particularly since it was sheep-shearing time, when there would have been plenty to spare. (Note that there was plenty for a lavish feast in v 36, also v 18.)

5. Look at the way Nabal responds (v 10-11). What exactly makes him a fool?
Nabal clearly knows who David is ("son of Jesse" v 10). He is rude, mean, ill-informed, disrespectful and insulting. But the heart of Nabal's folly is that he treats the LORD's anointed with such contempt. In rejecting God's anointed, he is rejecting God Himself.

If your group are struggling, ask:
- **What was special about David?** He was the LORD's anointed—see introduction on page 37 of the study guide.
- **How did Nabal's treatment of David reveal more than just contempt for a man he did not care for?** By treating the LORD's anointed with contempt, Nabal was showing contempt for God, who had chosen David.

6. Is David's reaction reasonable? Why/why not (v 12-13, 21-22)?

- **Was David's anger justified?**
- **Did his reaction show a concern for justice and fairness?**

David's anger is partly justified. David had treated Nabal's men well (v 15) but Nabal has indeed returned evil for good (v 21) and he has not shown respect to the LORD's anointed. However, David is impetuous and fails to show restraint. It is only Abigail's quick actions that save him from needless bloodshed.

7. What qualities does Abigail show in what she does (v 14-23)?
She demonstrates her wisdom by listening to what Nabal's men say (v 14-17); acting quickly; wisely using the resources at her disposal to save the situation; recognising David as the LORD's anointed; being resourceful, practical, clever, humble and godly. She recognises what's important and stops David from getting side-tracked by his own petty battles.

8. How does she show good judgement in what she says to David (v 24-31)?
In the humble way she is prepared to take the blame on herself and ask for pardon (v 24); she recognises the truth about her husband; she affirms David's kingship; she sees the importance of keeping David from sin and unnecessary bloodshed. Look at the way she repeatedly refers to the LORD—pleasing Him and fulfilling His purposes are important to her.

There are several tricky phrases in this section. "My lord" (v 25 etc) refers to David and shows how Abigail responds to him as the LORD's anointed; "may your enemies … be like Nabal" (v 26)—this probably anticipates Nabal's death and is therefore a wish that all David's enemies would meet the same end; "someone is pursuing you" (v 29) presumably refers to Saul (24 v 2 etc). "bundle of the living" ie: the "book of life" (v 29)—Abigail reassures David that his salvation will be secure.

EXPLORE MORE
Read 2 Samuel 7 v 11-16 and Psalm 2. These words were originally spoken to or about David, the LORD's anointed. In what ways do they also speak of Jesus and point to Him? The whole of the Old Testament points to the Lord Jesus. Jesus is God's solution to the problem of human sin and its consequences; He is the long-awaited Messiah and the ultimate King. (For more on this, read *Gospel & Kingdom* by Graham Goldsworthy.)
In this session it is important to see how David points ahead to Jesus, because it shows us how we can apply the teaching of this passage. We do not copy Abigail exactly in what she does (ie: we do not acknowledge David as the LORD's anointed), but we draw out principles, such as acknowledging the LORD's anointed, and try to follow them.
2 Samuel 7 v 11b-16: A promise from the LORD to David, through Nathan the prophet. Look at what God promises to David. These promises are fulfilled for David, but even more completely for Jesus (eg: v 16).
Psalm 2: This coronation psalm of David, describing the role of the LORD's anointed king and his special relationship with God, is mentioned a number of times in the NT with reference to Jesus, or fulfilled by the events of His life (eg: v 1—Acts 4 v 25-28; v 7— Matthew 3 v 17; Acts 13 v 32-33, Hebrews 1 v 5; 5 v 5, 9—Revelation 19 v 15).

See also Psalm 22. How were these bitter experiences of David reflected in the life of Jesus? These words are spoken by David about himself and his own experiences. However, they are ultimately fulfilled in the death of the Lord Jesus. Notice how these words, spoken hundreds of years before crucifixion had even been invented, describe Jesus' experiences accurately and dramatically. Jesus spoke the words of verse 1 as He was being crucified (Matthew 27 v 46).
Why did God's ultimate King need to suffer in this way? For anyone in the group who does not yet understand the good news about Jesus, this would be an opportunity to talk about how Jesus' death is the only way to save us from our sins. (See also the prayer to make Jesus our King, suggested at the end of this session.)

9. APPLY: What lessons can we learn from the way that Abigail treated David, about how we need to approach God's greater King, the Lord Jesus Christ? Go back over what has been discussed in Q7+8, which also applies when we turn to Jesus to be saved from our sin, eg: the fact that Abigail lost no time in making peace, recognising David as the LORD's anointed and seeking to please him, asking for pardon, and becoming his bride.

• **How should this be reflected when we speak about Jesus to non-Christians, and explain what a Christian is?** Christians sometimes give the impression that Jesus is simply the best friend we can ever have, always there for us, ready to help us out of any trouble. While it is true that Jesus loves His people deeply and that Christians can come to Him at any time, He is much, much more than this—nothing less than God's appointed

King of the universe, to whom, one day every knee will bow (Philippians 2 v 9-11). A Christian is not just a nice person with religious interests; rather, someone who willingly bows the knee in submission to the Lord Jesus, trusting and obeying everything He has said. We need to make sure that this is what we communicate to others, both by our words and in the way we live our lives.

- **What does this teach us about true wisdom, and how different is this to the world's understanding of wisdom? (See 1 Corinthians 1 v 20-25; Colossians 2 v 2-3; 2 Timothy 3 v 15.)** Wisdom is found in Jesus Christ (Colossians 2 v 2-3), in understanding what He did on the cross (1 Corinthians 1 v 20-25) and in hearing and putting into practice His word (2 Timothy 3 v 15). True wisdom is to submit to God's King and be saved from our sin, so that we can be at peace with God—it's nothing to do with a fine education, academic qualifications or clever ideas. Wise people become Christians—foolish people don't!

10. What does David praise God for (v 32-34, 39)? He recognises that Abigail's good judgement is a gift from the LORD. He praises Him for this because it has kept him from sin. David's second prayer of praise is that justice has been done to Nabal.

11. How does the story end for David, Abigail and Nabal? David spares Nabal's household and acquires a wise, beautiful and politically useful wife in Abigail. Abigail's request (v 31) is granted. Nabal dies of a heart attack, which is seen as the LORD's judgment (v 38).

12. Look at Abigail's achievements—a successful peacemaker who saved her household from disaster and kept David from serious sin. What qualities helped Abigail to achieve these things? Wisdom, decisiveness, humility, bravery, practicality, eloquence, and an ability to think quickly.

- **Are these qualities characteristics that we either have or don't have—or can we develop them (see 2 Peter 1 v 3-9)? If so, how?** 2 Peter 1 v 3-9 shows us that godly qualities can and should be developed in those who have been cleansed from past sins, if we trust in God's power (v 3), take hold of His great and precious promises (v 4), make every effort to develop these qualities (v 5) and do not forget what Christ has done for us (v 9). In thinking of how to develop these qualities, try to come up with specific and practical suggestions. A couple of examples… Humility: could you pray every day for the next week that God would make you more humble? Bravery: what about resolving that next time someone asks what you did at the weekend, you tell them you went to church rather than talking about other things?

- **What could have stopped Abigail from taking action to prevent David from sinning? What stops us from caring for one another in this way (see James 5 v 20)?** Fear of how David might respond could have deterred Abigail from trying to dissuade David from sinning. Any such misgivings would have been unwarranted—this was the very thing that most impressed David (v 33-34). Abigail showed an ability to see the bigger picture behind this immediate situation (God's purposes through David—not just saving her own skin) and a commitment to David's true welfare (his godliness—not his feelings). Allow people to share reasons why they find this kind of intervention difficult, and practical suggestions on how we can carry out the instruction of James 5 v 20 graciously.

PRAY

If someone makes use of the prayer at the end of the session, suggest that they tell a Christian friend, who can encourage them as they start their Christian life. You could mention this at the start of the next session.

OPTIONAL EXTRA

How can Christians always be prepared in any place and at any time to help others become "wise for salvation"? Something that many Christians have found helpful is memorising a brief summary of the gospel, such as *Jesus. Who, Why... So What?* or *Two Ways to Live: The Choice We All Face.* Why not try reading one of these booklets like this and committing it to memory? Then, having prayed for non-Christians that you know, you can try it out on them. It may start some great conversations about the Christian faith, and you will be ready and able to explain what Christianity is all about whenever an opportunity arises. (Both resources are available from www. thegoodbook.co.uk / www.thegoodbook. com.)

7 2 Kings 4 v 8-37
THE SHUNAMMITE: FROM DEATH TO LIFE

THE BIG IDEA

A desperate woman pins her hopes on God's prophet and experiences God's awesome power.

SUMMARY

This episode takes place during the ministry of Elisha, before unfaithful Israel is taken into exile. It is one of four miracles in 2 Kings chapter 4, in which God uses Elisha to help His people in various hopeless situations. In this passage, we see the greatest miracle of all as God brings the Shunammite woman's dead son back to life.

GUIDANCE ON QUESTIONS

1. Do you know anyone who has come through a difficult situation? How would you judge that they had handled it well? What attitude to God would you look for? Possible answers may include: managing to keep looking outward; staying cheerful; not blaming God. (And for Christians) persisting with prayer; maintaining a concern for evangelism; using their experience to help others; forgiveness. A common but inadequate method of coping is to suppress or deny our feelings and perform in the way that we think is expected of a Christian. Ultimately, however, the facade will crack and the reality will be revealed in our attitude to God, (distant, apathetic, resentful) and our lack of interest or failure in the tougher aspects of Christian living (prayer, forgiveness, and evangelism). This session deals with the authentic way to handle feelings of great desperation, distress and anger.

2. What do verses 8-10 tell us about this woman's situation and her faith?
The Shunammite is a rich, married, Israelite woman. She is generous, hospitable and capable. She is astute in recognising Elisha as someone special. She does not expect anything in return for her generosity. Her beliefs are not spelled out at the beginning, but she clearly recognises Elisha is a "holy man of God" and she treats him with great honour and respect.

3. How does Elisha try to reward the woman and thank her for her kindness (v 11-16a)? He asks whether she needs royal or military protection (v 13). She replies that she is content to live among her own people (although she will in fact need this type of help later—2 Kings 8 v 1-6). Gehazi suggests that the woman would like a son.

4. Look at the woman's answers to Elisha in verses 13b and 16b. In what way are they different? Why does she react as she does? In v 13b the woman is self-reliant and content. In v 16b, she is politely sceptical (along the lines of "you must be joking!"). She clearly has become resigned to remaining childless. This is not dissimilar to Sarah's reaction in Genesis 18 v 11-12. While the first response seems to be that of true contentment, the second shows an unwillingness to take Elisha's (and therefore God's) words on trust. She has probably spent many years struggling with her desire to have children. Having more or less come to terms with the situation, she is reluctant to have her hopes raised again.

EXPLORE MORE
… Why is this son given? What does this show about God's character? Purely for motherly enjoyment. God delights to give

us good gifts and we see the simplicity of His goodness here.

5. APPLY: How do we show the same tendency [afraid to hope, in case we're disappointed] eg: in our prayers, our relationships and our evangelism?
Prayer: Perhaps the group would be willing to share examples of prayers that they have been afraid to pray, in case God didn't give what they had requested. (It would also be encouraging to hear examples of answered prayers, made to God originally in fear and trepidation.)
Relationships: Difficult or damaged relationships with spouses, parents, children and other Christians frequently drift along unsatisfactorily because of our fears of what will happen if we pray or act for change. These are more personal issues, which people may find difficult to talk about in the group, but attention should be drawn to the importance of thinking through personal challenges in this area.
Evangelism: Discuss how Christians might fail to witness to a non-Christian person because we fear a hostile reaction. Or, when we try to organise evangelism, how much time can be spent agonising over possible failure, instead of just getting on with Christ's command to go and make disciples. Get people to think about the reasons why we are like this.

- **What is the root cause of this kind of refusal to ask for God's help?** The reason we protect ourselves from possible painful disappointment is because we don't believe God is either able or willing to help us. Perhaps we feel too sinful, and have forgotten that God treats His children according to grace, not according to how well we have done (Romans 5 v 2). Perhaps we don't understand that He loves to give His children good gifts (Matthew 7 v 9-12). At the root of our self-protection is lack of faith in God's character and/or power.

- **What do we miss out on if we simply continue to put up with existing circumstances?** We will miss out on the good things that God wants to give us (Matthew 7 v 9-12), which means missing out on an opportunity to learn how amazingly powerful and loving our heavenly Father really is. So we won't be able to grow in our faith and delight in Him, or have stories of His goodness that we can share with others.

6. What qualities does the woman show in the way she deals with her son's illness and death (v 18-25a)? Her son suffers an illness (perhaps heatstroke or meningitis). Showing tender motherly care, she looks after him until he dies (v 20). She lays him on the prophet's bed (perhaps putting the responsibility for his death on Elisha?). She keeps calm. She heads straight for the man of God at Mount Carmel, about 20 miles away. The significance of her husband's question (v 23) is that such visits would usually be kept for rest days.

7. In what ways does Elisha show sensitivity and understanding (v 25b-27)? He spots her. He sends his servant to check how she is. (Again she says: "Everything is all right"—"shalom", v 26b—because she wants to speak directly to the man of God herself.) Elisha senses the pain and hurt beneath her words; he stops Gehazi pushing her away and does not rebuke her for her outburst. He is modest and humble in admitting that the LORD has not revealed the problem to him.

8. Re-read verses 27-28. What do you think the woman is feeling as she asks the question in verse 28? The Shunammite woman is now desperate. She clings to Elisha's feet (v 27). Her question is angry and accusing. She had not asked him for a son. The implication is that it would have been better not to have had the son at all, than to have had him and lose him so quickly. She lays the blame clearly at the feet of the prophet.

9. How does this woman show faith? Despite her angry accusations, the woman shows faith by coming straight to the man of God. Faith is not a matter feelings but of what we do despite our feelings.

10. What is the contrast in verses 29-37 between God and His servants, Gehazi and Elisha? God's servants are limited in their powers and abilities: Gehazi is unable to bring the boy back to life; Elisha succeeds—but only through prayer. In verse 27 we saw how the LORD had not revealed the situation to Elisha. (The strange action of v 34 is similar to Elijah in 1 Kings 17 v 21. It is not meant to imply resuscitation, as the boy was clearly dead. But although God could have brought about this miracle without human agency, He instead chooses to involve His prophet in it.) Note that God's servants are always limited and we should not expect them to be perfect. God Himself, by contrast, is seen to have limitless power. Not even death is a match for Him (see Romans 8 v 38-39), and He brings the boy back to life. In the other incidents in this chapter, we see God's power in miraculously providing oil, rescuing prophets from poisoned food and miraculously feeding 100 people. The gift of life is a very great gift— and, of course, the greatest gift of all, the gift of eternal life, is available to all of us.

11. Look back over the passage. What changes have there been in the way the woman responds to God and His prophet (contrast verses 8-10 and 13b with verses 27-28, 30 and 37)? The woman recognises that Elisha is a holy man of God (v 8-10), but at first, she has no sense of needing anything the prophet can offer her (v 13b). Later, in desperate need, she seeks the prophet's help urgently and blames him for her son's death (v 27-28); she is insistent that it is the prophet himself who helps her (v 30). At the end, she falls to the ground in awe and gratitude (v 37).

12. What good things come out of the tragedy? She sees her need, and she also sees God's amazing power at work.

EXPLORE MORE

Compare this story with that of the widow of Nain in Luke 7 v 11-17. What similarities and differences do you notice?
Similarities: The child was an only son; the mothers were desperate; each son was brought back to life and given back to the mother; the effect on the witnesses (the mother in 2 Kings 4 and the crowd in Luke 7) was one of awe; not even death puts someone beyond the voice of God; the incidents took place in the same geographical area—Shunem and Nain are only a couple of miles apart.
Differences: In Luke 7, the boy was dead in a coffin and the funeral procession was taking place. Elisha performed the miracle out of sight, whereas Jesus was in full view of the crowd. Elisha prayed that God would act, whereas Jesus spoke directly to the corpse. Elisha is merely God's servant, but Jesus is God in human form.
The raising of the Shunammite woman's son is a preview of what Jesus would

do several hundred years later. And Jesus' miracle is a preview of what (see John 11 v 25)? The fact that He is the resurrection and the life, and those that believe in Him will never truly die (ie: suffer God's eternal punishment).

13. APPLY: How might this passage help someone who feels angry with God for the way things have turned out? In particular, what have you learned about... For someone who is angry, it is helpful to recognise that faith is not always serene. Trusting God doesn't mean gliding effortlessly through difficulties.

- **God's character and the way He works?** This incident shows that God is powerful. Nothing is too great for Him to deal with—even death. He is generous and delights to give good gifts to His people. He does answer prayer (although we clearly cannot assume that God will always answer prayers in the way that we want Him to). God uses His servants to carry out His plans. This story also reminds us that God is beyond our understanding—we do not always understand His purposes. Sometimes we may understand after the event; sometimes we may not.

- **faith? Do the woman's angry feelings show that she lacked faith?** Faith is shown by our actions, not our feelings. The woman was angry and accusing—but, in her desperation, she put her trust in God's prophet.

- **the reasons why God may allow us to suffer devastating experiences?** There are many reasons why God allows Christians to suffer tragedies: to strengthen our faith (1 Peter 1 v 6-7); to discipline us (Hebrews 12 v 7-9); to enable us to help others (2 Corinthians 1 v 4); and, as in this story, to reveal God's amazing power. You could suggest that members focus on one aspect of God's character and think how that might affect their daily lives.

OPTIONAL EXTRA
Most of us struggle, not only with making time to pray, but also with what to pray about once we have set aside some time for it. If your mind goes blank at this point, a useful tool is a prayer diary. A prayer diary can include the following:
• a checklist for daily prayer, helping us to pray according to the pattern that Jesus gave us in the Lord's Prayer (eg: praise God for things learned in Bible-reading, thanks for blessings and answered prayers,

confession, and requests).
• a checklist for weekly or monthly prayer, so that we ask God's help for a range of people/activities (eg: missionaries, Sunday school teachers and youth leaders, the person who will be teaching at church on Sunday, our neighbours, work-colleagues and friends, persecuted Christians etc.).
• a section for short-term prayer requests (eg: an up-and-coming evangelistic event, a fellow Christian in a difficult situation).
This week's project is to organise a prayer diary or folder that will help you to pray regularly, widely, and biblically. For more ideas on this, see *A Call to Spiritual Reformation* by Don Carson.

---

8 Proverbs 31 v 10-31
THE GODLY WIFE:
FROM WISDOM TO HONOUR

THE BIG IDEA
We are given a portrait of a godly woman, who fears the LORD. This is expressed in her character, her relationships and the way she uses her gifts and resources.

SUMMARY
The big theme of Proverbs is "wisdom"—everyday, down-to-earth wisdom. This passage is a description of what wisdom would look like in the home. Since it is an acrostic poem (each verse beginning with a different letter of the Hebrew alphabet), there is no obvious structure. The passage describes this woman's character, the way she cares for her husband and children, manages her home, responds to the needs of others, how she carries out her business

affairs, etc. Her motivation is seen clearly in verse 30—she fears the LORD.

GUIDANCE ON QUESTIONS
1. What qualities do you admire in women that you know? Make a list together of the qualities that are admired in our culture. Although the passage describes a married woman, there are lessons for all of us. This initial question is designed to broaden the scope of the discussion and to prevent those who are not married women from feeling that this passage has nothing to say to them.

2. Glance over the whole passage and make a list of the different people and activities this woman is involved with.

The passage describes how she carries out her roles of wife, mother, running the household, businesswoman, neighbour etc.

3. What is the evidence that this woman is a great wife and mother? She cares for her husband and children in her well-managed home (see v 10-12, 15, 21-23, 26-29.) Phrases that may need further explanation: "lacks nothing of value" (v 11)—her husband benefits from how well she runs the household; "scarlet" (v 21)—the translation is uncertain, and means either "scarlet" (ie: expensive) or "double" (ie: double thickness, warm); "coverings … linen … purple" (v 22)—the bedding and clothes are good quality; "city gate" (v 23)—the centre of political life, meaning that she sets her husband free to be involved in public life; "wisdom … faithful instruction" (v 26)—probably both to her children and her friends; v 29 is probably what her husband says about her.

4. How does this compare with what the world tells us is important? The world applauds and promotes success and self-fulfilment, rather than assistance and service of others; public recognition rather than behind-the-scenes involvement; a career outside the home rather than unpaid work in the home etc. But God commends unrecognised acts of service and sacrifice, and sees the secret motivation of our hearts. You may be able to tie in this contrast with the discussions arising out of Q1.

5. What is striking about the way she runs her business affairs? She has considerable skills as a businesswoman (see verses 13-14, 16-19, 24). "Merchant ships … food from afar" (v 14)—she is a skilful and enterprising businesswoman; "lamp" (v 18)—it is still alight either because she

is hardworking and still busy late into the night, or because she is prosperous and can afford to keep it alight; "distaff" (v 19)—probably means that she is skilled at making her own thread. She has a prosperous home (servants, money to invest, etc) and she makes the most of her opportunities and resources.

6. How does she treat the poor? She does not keep her success to herself and her family, but cares for the poor and needy (see v 20).

EXPLORE MORE
Compare the ideal wife with the woman called "Wisdom" (see Proverbs 3 v 13-18, 4 v 5-9 and 9 v 1-6). What similarities can you find? Compare... 3 v 13-15 with 31 v 10—more precious than rubies; 4 v 6 with 31 v 12 & 27—protection and watchfulness; 4 v 8 with 31 v 23—honour and respect; 9 v 6 with 31 v 26—faithful teaching. Proverbs 3 v 13-18 portrays the woman called "Wisdom" as someone who brings prosperity and a pleasant life—similarly, the family described in Proverbs 31 represent a lifestyle that most people would aspire to and recognise as "the good life", making the point that wisdom brings fulfilment and satisfaction. Proverbs 4 v 5-9 shows that wisdom will protect from harm and bring honour—similarly, the ideal wife works hard to protect her household from hunger, poverty and the cold, and her husband is respected because of her. Proverbs 9 v 1-6 describes the feast of understanding that wisdom provides—similarly, the ideal wife is busy faithfully instructing others. We can conclude that the woman called "Wisdom" and the ideal wife of Proverbs 31 are the same. From this we are meant to understand that the ideal wife is also an embodiment of wisdom, giving us

an example of what wisdom looks like when it is lived out, in this case, in the home. The ultimate example of wisdom lived out is, of course, Christ (see next Explore More below).

Who is the teaching about wisdom for? The teaching on wisdom in the early chapters of Proverbs is addressed to young men for whom this book was written (eg: 3 v 11, 4 v 1 etc.). But it is not only for them (Proverbs 31 is all about a woman)—it is for all people, who want to live wisely.

What about the teaching about the ideal wife? So, it seems reasonable to assume that the teaching of Proverbs 31 isn't intended for married women only, but for everyone who wants to be wise (see Q9 below). **Why do you think wisdom is "personified" like this in Proverbs? (See Matthew 11 v 19 and James 1 v 22-25—what do these passages show us about wisdom in the Bible?)** Wisdom is personified in Proverbs to show us what it means to be wise in everyday life—wisdom is not mystical, mysterious or even religious; it's doing ordinary things in a way that is shaped by our "fear of the LORD" (9 v 10). Matthew 11 v 19 indicates that wisdom is shown by what we do, and James 1 v 22-25 underlines that knowledge, even from God's word, is useless if it is not put into practice.

7. If beauty is "fleeting" (v 30), why do we find it so appealing? Discuss why charm is deceptive and beauty is fleeting, and how much we are taken in by the world's preoccupation with youth and beauty. These things appeal to us because the world applauds them and because sinful human nature responds to what we see, rather than putting value on, and faith in, what is unseen ie: God. Physical beauty is not dismissed in the Bible (it is celebrated in Song of Songs). But charm and beauty

do not last and they can be faked with cosmetics and plastic surgery, whereas the fear of the LORD lasts for eternity.

8. Why is "a woman who fears the LORD" to be praised (v 30)? Discuss the meaning of "fearing" the LORD—ie: not being frightened of Him, but responding to Him with a loving, submissive, obedient reverence. (Here it may be helpful to recap Q7 of Session 3.) This is what lasts and what really matters in life, because true "fear of the LORD" makes us seek His grace and mercy in Jesus, through whom we receive forgiveness and eternal life.

9. APPLY: This passage is all about a married woman. What principles of wise living can you find that would be relevant to other people? Whether we are male or female, married or unmarried, we should all fear the LORD (v 30) because this is the beginning of wisdom (1 v 7). It is then up to each individual Christian to work out what everyday, down-to-earth wisdom will look like in their situation. Principles may include being a "people person", putting the interests of others first, working hard, being prepared for the future, making oneself responsible to help whoever is in need etc. Note: the teaching about the ideal wife can also help us pray for and encourage our married female friends. (For example, don't comment on their new clothes, but instead, comment on their godliness or service). And it teaches men what to value in women (especially v 30).

• **What is the link between the "fear of the LORD" (v 30) and wisdom? See Proverbs 1 v 7; 2 v 1-6; 9 v 10; 15 v 33; Psalm 111 v 10; Job 28 v 28.** The fear of the LORD is the beginning of wisdom—ie: the starting point, but also the main goal.

- **How can we follow the instruction of Proverbs 4 v 7 to "get wisdom"?**
By listening to, accepting and storing up God's word, and investing time and effort in understanding it (Proverbs 2 v 1-6); by following what God tells us to do (Psalm 111 v 10); by turning away from evil (Job 28 v 28).

EXPLORE MORE
Read Col 2 v 2-3 and 1 Cor 1 v 30. What does the New Testament add to our understanding of wisdom? If we want to know what wisdom is now we need to look at Jesus Christ, "in whom are hidden all the treasures of wisdom and knowledge" (Colossians 2 v 2-3) and "who has become for us wisdom from God" (1 Corinthians 1 v 30).
Who is the ultimate ideal human (1 John 3 v 5)? Jesus is—"in him is no sin".
Read Romans 8 v 28-30 and 1 John 3 v 2-3. Can Christians ever achieve the perfection represented by this ideal wife? How can these verses be an encouragement? Romans 8 v 29 tells us that God has predestined those He has chosen to become like His Son, and 1 John 3 v 2 tells Christians that when Jesus returns, they will be like Him. Christians can be encouraged by these verses because they tell us that, however remote the prospect may seem now, one day all God's people will be perfect as Jesus is, and it is this hope that motivates Christians to purify themselves from sin (1 John 3 v 3).

10. APPLY: Now that Jesus has come to our world and we live in the age of the gospel (we can know the good news about Jesus), what does it mean today to fear the LORD and live wisely (see Luke 12 v 5 and 2 Timothy 3 v 15)? Jesus tells us that we should fear God alone, if only for the fact that He has power over body and soul and can throw us into hell (Luke 12 v 5). The implications of this "fear of the LORD" are that we should seek God's forgiveness, which comes through Jesus Christ. 2 Timothy 3 v 15 tells us that we can be made wise by finding salvation through faith in Christ Jesus. So, in the age of the gospel, wisdom = becoming a Christian.

11. APPLY: Read Galatians 6 v 9-10; 1 Corinthians 15 v 58; Colossians 3 v 16 and 1 Peter 3 v 15; 1 Thessalonians 5 v 1-11. How can a Christian put into practice the principles of wise living found in Proverbs 31? For a Christian, principles of wise living include… caring for God's family of Christian brothers and sisters (Galatians 6 v 9-10); giving ourselves fully to the work of the Lord (1 Corinthians 15 v 58); teaching God's word to fellow Christians (Colossians 3 v 16)—this can be done informally and one to one in private conversation—and explaining the Christian message to interested non-Christians (1 Peter 3 v 15); preparing ourselves and encouraging others to be ready for the return of our Lord Jesus Christ (1 Thessalonians 5 v 1-11). Maybe your group can think of other examples. Take time to discuss what each would mean in practice.

12. APPLY: Read Titus 2 v 3-5. What are the similarities with Proverbs 31? What motivates a Christian woman to live like this? (see also v 8 and 10)? In what way can our motives be sinful? Titus 2 v 3-5 talks about women teaching and training other women (cf. Proverbs 31 v 26); loving husbands and children (cf. v 12, 15, 28); being busy in the home (cf. v 15, 17, 18, 27); being kind (cf. v 20). The motivation is that no one will malign the word of God (Titus 2 v 5). In this chapter of his letter to

Titus, Paul repeatedly urges Christians to live godly lives so that non-Christians will be attracted to the gospel, or at least they will have no excuse for rejecting it (see Titus 2 v 8 and 10). So Christians have a special motive for living wisely—their desire to help people turn to Jesus Christ. Discuss the difference between this and sinful motives such as perfectionism, pleasing or impressing other people, competitiveness etc. Think of the people you relate to and the activities you are involved with; then make a list of, say, five characteristics/qualities that should

mark you out as a follower of Jesus in your situation.

OPTIONAL EXTRA

One of the suggestions at the end of Session Four was about memorising parts of Scripture. Has anyone in your group tried that yet? What about learning a verse or two this week? Proverbs 31 v 30 would be a good one to start with. If you find memorising verses difficult, learning them with other people often helps

Good Book Guides
A selection from the range

the**good**book
COMPANY
Opening up the Bible

At The Good Book Company, we are dedicated to helping Christians and local churches grow. We believe that God's growth process always starts with hearing clearly what he has said to us through his timeless word—the Bible.

Ever since we opened our doors in 1991, we have been striving to produce resources that honour God in the way the Bible is used. We have grown to become an international provider of user-friendly resources to the Christian community, with believers of all backgrounds and denominations using our Bible studies, books, evangelistic resources, DVD-based courses and training events.

We want to equip ordinary Christians to live for Christ day by day, and churches to grow in their knowledge of God, their love for one another, and the effectiveness of their outreach.

Call us for a discussion of your needs or visit one of our local websites for more information on the resources and services we provide.

Your friends at The Good Book Company

UK & EUROPE    thegoodbook.co.uk   0333 123 0880
NORTH AMERICA   thegoodbook.com   866 244 2165
AUSTRALIA   thegoodbook.com.au   (02) 9564 3555
NEW ZEALAND   thegoodbook.co.nz   (+64) 3 343 2463

 WWW.CHRISTIANITYEXPLORED.ORG
Our partner site is a great place for those exploring the Christian faith, with a clear explanation of the good news, powerful testimonies and answers to difficult questions.